to the PRAISE of HIS GLORY

A radical approach
to worship
and the
worshipper

D1627682

DAVE FELLINGHAM
Foreword by Terry Virgo

KINGSWAY PUBLICATIONS
EASTBOURNE

DEDICATION

To a wonderful family.

To the memory of a Dad, who knew how to express love and who established spiritual foundations in my life.

To a Mum whose voice still rings with love for Jesus.

To my wife, Rosie, who has lovingly seen me through many 'changing scenes of life'.

To my two sons, Luke and Nathan, who are following in my footsteps and pioneering prophetic vision into the next century.

Contents

Achnowledgements

I should like to thank Mary Austin for her hard work going through the material and preparing it for publication. She's displayed great patience!

I should also like to thank John Hosier and the full-time leadership team at Church of Christ the King in Brighton. My ideas, although well-intentioned, have sometimes been quite provocative, and the team have listened to, weighed and shaped them. The principles in this book work because these men have given me both freedom and boundaries. Their release and covering have given me great security.

Finally I should like to thank Terry Virgo, a man with apostolic wisdom and prophetic vision, who has had a profound influence on my life and ministry.

FOREWORD

I f you arrive in a town, how do you identify a true church there? What heads up your list of priorities? Do you look for people who believe in the atonement, who love one another, or who follow New Testament doctrine? The apostle Paul could have described the church in any of these ways, but he actually underlined another distinctive, 'We ... are the circumcision, we who worship by the Spirit of God, who glory in Christ Jesus, and who put no confidence in the flesh' (Phil 3:3). Spirit-inspired worship was top of his list. Above all else, God wants worship to characterise our lives. He seeks not only converts, but worshippers.

Sometimes we use the word 'worship' in a worldly setting. One day I was listening to a radio phone-in quiz programme. The presenter asked a guy maybe twenty detailed questions about a pop group and he answered every one correctly. I was amazed. He'd obviously filled his mind with this group. He'd bought their records and had their autographs. He went to their concerts and probably wore their sort of clothes. He 'worshipped' them.

Worship isn't simply about how we run the meeting. It's about being delighted with God. It isn't about attending a meeting for an hour or so on a Sunday. It's about being a worshipper all day, every day. We are called to an everlasting preoccupation with God.

God is looking for worshippers who will worship him in Spirit and truth. I believe that he's finding increasing numbers of them. As the Holy Spirit sweeps through the church, he's drawing individuals into deeper intimacy with Jesus. We're meditating on his character and he's giving us greater security in him. Because our relationship with God is growing stronger, we're trusting and worshipping him more — even when we're going through real difficulties. We're also realising that all we do is an act of worship and want to honour him in every area of our lives.

The Spirit has been revolutionising our corporate worship too. Everywhere I go I encounter Christians of all ages praising God with real joy and enthusiasm. Unbelievers who come into meetings are amazed at the new life that's flowing and the worship that's taking place. They find that musty old hymns with language more appropriate to another generation are being replaced by vibrant new songs of praise and worship.

Often churches are singing songs written by Dave Fellingham, a personal friend and colleague of mine whose songs and whole approach to worship I greatly value. He has not only been given a wonderful gift of musical composition, he also has a worshipping heart and a love for Scripture. Again and again I find myself approaching God with his songs on my lips and in my heart.

Dave takes worship seriously and is uniquely qualified to offer this book to the Christian public for their blessing and enrichment. I thank God for him and his great contribution to the worshipping church in our generation.

Terry Virgo

PREFACE

In recent years I've had many opportunities to teach on praise and worship in churches and at conferences around the world. Much of the material in this book has been drawn from my lectures and seminars, and also from my last book, *Worship Restored*.

The more I've taught, the more I've realised that it's impossible to separate worship from any other aspect of the Christian life. Our goal is to love God, know him and glorify him in everything we do — whether in evangelism, prayer, spiritual warfare and church planting, or in our personal relationships, at our workplace, in our home and in our social lives. So I find it very difficult to teach on worship without reverence to God's purpose for the church, revival, personal wholeness and our eternal destiny.

To the praise of his glory is a book which deals with a variety of subjects — but from the perspective of our being worshippers. It's personal in that it covers my own spiritual pilgrimage and it's pastoral because it highlights many issues that I've encountered in several years of pastoral care. Many people find it hard to abandon themselves in worship because of past hurts and bad experiences.

There's also a prophetic dimension to the book. I'm very grateful to God for my relationships within New Frontiers and the prophetic thrust that comes from a vision for the restoration of the church. I have a passionate commitment to seeing church life filled with God's power and glory, and functioning as God intended from the beginning — a church which is experiencing his presence and is communicating with a dying world.

Dave Fellingham

CHAPTER 1

a HEART *for* WORSHIP

I stood on the platform at the Olympic Stadium in Seoul, Korea and gazed out at 80,000 people. Minutes before, they'd been singing a song that I'd composed in my front room to express my own love for God. Now, thousands knew it. In fact, as I'd gone into the Stadium people were walking along singing other songs that I'd written. I was so moved and excited. I could never have dreamed that one day my songs would go around the world; that God would use me to stir the hearts of his people to worship.

My life has always revolved around music. I was born in 1945 in Horsham, Sussex and my parents were officers in the Salvation Army. We soon moved from Horsham to Little Lever in Greater Manchester and then to the village of Tongham near Farnham, Surrey, where I spent most of my childhood. My parents were based in the Salvation Army corps in Aldershot, which they helped to run, and Dad preached round the local churches and in open airs. In the late '40s and early '50s God's Spirit moved in the Aldershot corps and many young people were converted.

Sunday was a very busy day in my family. It often started with a 7.00am prayer meeting, then continued with the 10.00am open air meeting and the 11.00am holiness meeting. After a quick lunch we returned for the 2.00pm open air meeting and the 3.00pm praise and testimony meeting. After a quick tea we were back for the 6.00pm open air meeting, the 7.00pm gospel meeting and the prayer meeting which immediately followed it. Then we all went home and had supper, which was usually bubble and squeak made with the leftovers from lunch. Even though it was late by then, we often gathered around the piano for a family worship time — which was always very special.

Of course, the Salvation Army is known for its music, its brass bands and hymns, and its emphasis on evangelism and bringing in the kingdom of God. At the Sunday night salvation meeting the band played, we sang hymns (called 'songs' in the Salvation Army), the Songster Brigade sang and someone preached the gospel. Then we had the prayer meeting. People were encouraged to pray aloud, read the scriptures and start up songs. These prayer meetings had a tremendous impact on me — right from the tender age of four or five — because we often experienced a wonderful sense of the presence of God.

My grandfather lived with us during my early childhood. He was converted in the late nineteenth century and had a remarkable zeal for God. He used to go round in a gypsy caravan preaching the gospel from one village to another. Then he went to the Salvation Army training college and became a Salvation Army Officer. Before he was married, he and another Salvation Army officer called Captain Gumbleton were sent to one place and lived in the same house. The two of them prayed for everyone in their road and saw them all converted. When the local council heard about this they actually changed the name of the street to Salvation Row.

His diary records that on one occasion he was sent to Hull to take command of the Salvation Army corps there. On the journey he decided that he was going to begin with half nights of prayer — which was exactly what the people in Hull had already proposed to do. Numbers at these half nights of prayer began at twenty and dropped to five, where they remained for many weeks. Then the people returned and revival broke out. They went out with their musical instruments, raided public houses at midnight and saw many conversions. My grandfather went from Hull to Royston, where he 'saved a man from hanging' — whatever that meant. Clearly he was mightily used by God.

When I was very young he was quite elderly, but I can still remember watching him in the Salvation Army meetings. He'd raise his hands in worship, or link arms with another old man in the congregation and dance around with him. When he was at home, he was always singing, playing his concertina and praising God. He was full of joy and the power of the Spirit, and he had a wonderful influence on me.

So our house was filled with worship and Christian service and everything revolved around the Salvation Army. During the week there was the band practice, the choir practice, the Bible study, other midweek meetings and the Saturday open air. My father also went out with the magazine, War Cry, and evangelised in the pubs. Family life was very busy, but we really enjoyed it and were thoroughly involved in it too.

My parents brought me up to love the Bible and pray, so I always believed in God and was often conscious of his presence. But one day when I was eight years old I went forward at a children's meeting, knelt at the 'penitent form' and gave my life to Jesus. By this time, I was learning the cornet and the piano and singing with my sister and parents. My interest in music was beginning to grow.

In 1954 my parents took me to hear Billy Graham at Harringay. Even though I was only nine years old, the event had a great impact on me. The atmosphere was wonderful and the streets were packed with singing people. I'll never forget Billy Graham's appeal and the choir singing the old gospel hymn, 'Just as I am.' I know that he's often been criticised for emotionalism, but I just revelled in God's presence. And I began to see how music could soften people's hearts.

When I was about eleven years old I became interested in pop music — which was very different then from what it is now. Rock and roll was coming in — with singers like Tommy Steele, Bill Hayley and the Comets and Elvis Presley. But the kind of music that really caught my attention was skiffle, which comprised folk music and rock and roll. The combination of the guitar, tea chest bass and washboard gave this music a very earthy rhythmic drive and I really got into it — as did most of my friends. Suddenly I had a tremendous desire to get a guitar and learn how to play.

My parents bought me my first guitar when I was twelve years old. At that time, the famous skiffle artist in the UK was Lonny Donnegan and I learnt how to play one of his songs — 'I shall not be moved' — with the chords of G, C and D7. My father, who wasn't a great fan of this kind of music, heard me practising and said to me, 'Do you know that those words are like Psalm 1? That Psalm speaks about being like a securely planted tree which can't be moved.' I immediately adapted Lonny Donnegan's song and sang it at the Salvation Army meeting the following Sunday.

I was used to doing things in public — praying in meetings, playing the cornet in the Army band and giving my testimony — but this was the first time that I'd ever sung to the guitar. Before long I was regularly taking old hymns, rearranging them in a skiffle style and playing them in the Salvation Army meetings and open airs. Some people hated the new style of worship, but in the main it was quite popular. At that time, praising God with a guitar was rather a radical thing to do. Few Christians had guitars or knew how to play them, and suddenly people began asking me to sing and play in their local churches.

Our piano was in the front room and I'd often sit at it, sing hymns and learn to play them by heart. It was during those times that I'd sense God's presence the most. One day, when I was still twelve years old, I was playing and singing a hymn about Jesus in Gethsemane. As I sang the words, 'That was my Lord who was praying for me,' I suddenly heard God speak to me. The sense of his presence was so strong that even our ever-tweeting canary was muted and a great hush descended on the room. That experience had a profound effect on me and I knew then that God was calling me to serve him in Christian ministry, whatever that meant.

My father taught me that I should always go to a meeting ready to speak, sing or pray in public. That training has lived with me and even now I go to every meeting prepared to receive and to give. I was about fourteen when Dad encouraged me not just to sing and play the guitar, but to speak as well. So from that time on, I started preaching. My first sermon was in the little Brethren chapel in the village where we lived.

My school education was chequered. I went to a Church of England junior school and was always among the top three in my class. I was expected to pass the 11+ exam and go to grammar school, but for some unknown reason, I failed it. My father made an incredible fuss and I took it again — and failed. After I'd failed it for the third time, I was packed off to the secondary modern school which had a very poor reputation. There were no external exam courses and there was a lot of bullying. My two years there were hard, but then I passed a 13+ exam and transferred to a school in Guildford.

This school was actually a technical school, a grammar school and a secondary modern school all under one roof. I was in the technical school learning about brickwork, woodwork, metalwork, plumbing, technical drawing and physics — but they really didn't suit my character. I was an artistic, creative person who enjoyed things like music and history. In this school, if you didn't get five O Levels you couldn't go into the sixth form. I ended up with one O Level in English and faced the prospect of retaking my fifth year.

My father believed that I was capable of much more, so he fought for me. He saw the headmaster and said, 'David is doing the wrong things. If you let him do the more arty subjects he'll do quite well.' He persuaded the headmaster to let me go into the sixth form where I beavered away at four more suitable O Levels and three A Levels. I passed the lot, which meant that I was able to go to university.

During my teenage years I developed my musical skills. I became a very competent cornet soloist and worked hard on the trumpet and guitar. I also began to gain a reputation as a singer and songwriter. God seemed to be showing me the close relationship between music, his presence and the preaching of the gospel. I discovered that when I played certain songs or hymns God drew really close to me and opened my heart to him.

Major Alistair Smith, the famous Keswick speaker, had a profound influence on me. When I was still a teenager, I'd sit spellbound under his passionate preaching on subjects like the cross, holiness and the second coming. I'd make as many notes as I could and then try and preach like him. By now, I was regularly speaking and singing in the open air. Sometimes I went out on the streets with my sister. One of us would preach and the other would heckle — just to draw a crowd.

In my late teens I met Rosemary Downer, who later became my wife. She was involved with the local Pentecostal church and I went along to some of the Sunday meetings there. I'd heard about the baptism and gifts of the Spirit, but I assumed that God had already given me his power and that the gifts had all died out with the early apostles. The trouble was that at these meetings I encountered prayer for the sick, speaking in tongues, interpretation of tongues, prophecy and deliverance. I'd read a lot about the way that the early Salvationists used to move in signs and wonders and it occurred to me that their founder, William Booth, wasn't against the gifts of the Spirit. In fact, he was very positive about them. Rosie and I used to debate about spiritual things and she gradually convinced me that God had much more in store for me. I began to seek the baptism of the Spirit.

After I left school I worked for a year in the public library in Aldershot. On my day off I used to spend time thirsting for more of God and reading every book that I could find on the baptism of the Spirit. One afternoon I was in my bedroom reading Andrew Murray's book, *The Spirit of Christ* when God's power suddenly fell on me. The experience dramatically affected my life. The first time that I preached after I'd received the baptism in the Spirit, twenty people came forward to receive Christ. I began speaking in tongues, prophesying and praying for the sick. It was a time of great spiritual activity and joy.

I became passionate and very bold about proclaiming my new-found experience. Since I was already reasonably well-known as a singer and guitarist, I had access to many churches which weren't particularly open to the things of the Spirit.

To put the message across, I wrote a song called, 'There was a man' and sang it wherever I went. The last verse goes,

> *These signs shall follow them that believe in me*
> *These words of the Lord are for all eternity.*
> *They shall speak new tongues when the Holy Ghost has*
> *come*
> *The sick shall be healed and the sinners brought home.*
> *These signs shall follow them that believe in me.*

It was about this time that Rosie and I formed a group called *The Witnesses*, which was a sort of Christian rock band. We had four vocals, a couple of guitars and sometimes a set of drums. We wrote our own songs and proclaimed the gospel in coffee bars, clubs and youth meetings. We were really zealous for God and had quite a lot of success. Evangelicals were beginning to warm to the idea of Christian bands and when Musical Gospel Outreach was formed, *The Witnesses* was one of the first groups on its list.

During that year in the public library I applied to the Royal College of Music to study the trumpet and was offered a place at another music college which offered an extremely good course. But for some reason I sensed that God wanted me to go to Brighton. I enrolled as a trainee teacher at what was then the Brighton College of Education, graduated from the University of Sussex with a Bachelor of Education degree and took my diploma in trumpet playing externally at the Royal College of Music.

While I was at college my musical development took a very positive turn. I was really interested in classical music and was in a local symphony orchestra. But now I was writing what might be described as contemporary classical music. By the time I'd graduated, I'd written two symphonies, two operas and a concerto and I was beginning to make a name for myself as a composer. My burning ambition was to become an orchestral conductor, but for now I was satisfied to be director of music at a high school in Brighton.

While I was teaching I wrote a piece of music called *New Creation* which was a cantata for symphony orchestra, rock band and choir. This was an unusual combination, a forerunner to other compositions by groups like Pink Floyd, Deep Purple and Emerson, Lake and Palmer. *New Creation* was considered a great breakthrough in the fusion of jazz, rock and classical music. It was featured on TV and discussed on the South Bank Show. It had excellent media coverage and I was hailed as an up and coming young composer who had something to say.

Unfortunately, this led to my becoming over-zealous in my musical career. I spent a lot of time playing in rock bands, dance bands, jazz bands, conducting orchestras and writing music, but satisfying as these things were, a void was beginning to open up inside me. I didn't deliberately rebel against God, it was more a case of his being crowded out because I was filling my life with musical activities. Success threatened my relationship with him.

One night I was in a trio, playing the piano in a night-club in Brighton. In the early hours of the morning God spoke to me using the words that he'd once said to Elijah: 'What are you doing here, David?' The phrase pierced my heart like an arrow. Suddenly I realised how far I'd drifted from him. I was still involved in an evangelical Church of England and on the following Sunday I joined the church for their morning meeting. We were singing 'Take my life and let it be consecrated Lord to thee.' As I sang, 'Take my voice and let me sing, ever only for my King,' God challenged me, 'Why are you using your musical gifts and skills to satisfy your own ambition when you should be using them to serve me?'

I knew that God had called me to serve him, but I was having such a satisfying life. I loved my job and my musical social life. I enjoyed playing in bands, rock groups and symphony orchestras and felt fulfilled writing compositions for many different kinds of instruments. I didn't want to give up my ambition and sort myself out. So there was a terrific struggle going on inside me. Rosie, by now my wife, was expecting the first of our two sons and I had to decide whether I was going to bring our children up with spiritual values. Finally I concluded that contentment could only be found in the will of God and I began to get my life back in order.

When the musical *Come Together* came to England, I went to the first performance at Westminster Central Hall. I didn't enjoy it much because I thought that the music was too simple. But God showed me that he anoints simple music and that I should stop trying to make everything as complicated as possible! I got back into church life and began to serve God again, but because music had become such a great diversion, I was very nervous about getting involved in it once more.

After I'd been teaching for seven years, I was invited to be assistant pastor at an Anglican Church where I stayed for two and a half years. At about this time God gave me a vision for a New Testament church in Brighton. Early one morning I was walking along Brighton beach, praying. The sun was rising and there was an early morning glow over the seafront buildings. Then God showed me a vision of a large church building, with hundreds of people, music and creativity. What struck me most was that it was a place where his glory was being manifested.

In 1978 I joined Terry Virgo who wanted to establish a church in the Brighton area. By that time, I was preaching again and becoming aware that something new was happening in worship. People like Graham Kendrick were writing songs that were expressing God's prophetic purposes. Christians were realising that the charismatic movement wasn't just for personal blessing — God was building his church and establishing his kingdom with power. As Terry preached on these values, they began to grip me and I started composing worship songs again. Originally they were meant just for the Brighton congregation — I'd prepare a sermon on a subject and if there wasn't an appropriate song, I'd write one to go with it. At the time, I had no idea that some of them would go around the world. That certainly wasn't my intention. All I wanted to do was write songs that helped people to worship and reinforced the preaching of God's word.

A few of my songs started getting quite popular. People would hear them in one place and take them back to their own local churches. That's how it started. Then, in 1980, I was invited to lead some of the worship at Downs Bible Week and suddenly my songs became much more widely known. The Downs live worship albums were a bit raw, but they had a real anointing and expressed in a fresh and exciting way how God was restoring his church. I was thrilled at the response to songs like, 'At your feet we fall' and 'Eternal God.' One evening I was in my living room. The nine o'clock news was on TV and someone was interviewing Billy Graham. I wasn't paying too much attention until I heard the song, 'God of glory' being sung in the background. I'd written that song in my front room for my local church and now the Billy Graham choir was singing it at peak viewing time and people were hearing it across the nation.

I was now an established song writer and worship leader — which meant that I was able to travel and experience praise and worship around the world. One day someone phoned me from Seoul, Korea and said that he wanted to meet me. Apparently, his local church had been singing one of my songs and God had begun to do something extraordinary. The song was, 'The Lord has displayed his glory' and there's a line in it which goes, 'Let the blind see, let the deaf hear, let the lame man leap like a deer.' He told me that as the people were singing these words, God was performing miracles among them. He just wanted to meet the person who'd written them. In 1991, he hired the Olympic Stadium in Seoul and asked me to speak at a worship conference there.

That was one of the most moving experiences that I've ever had. As we worshipped, the revival power of God swept like a mighty wind through entire sections of the Stadium. It was amazing. When I was on Prayer Mountain I experienced the presence of God and realised, more than ever before, the importance of prayer.

'Prayer Mountain' is about an hour's drive from Seoul. All over the hillside are small cells, each just large enough to accommodate one person. There are also large conference facilities. Every day, thousands of Christians get away from the routine of daily life and go to Prayer Mountain to spend time in prayer and fasting. As I drove up to the mountain, I was quite overwhelmed by the sound of prayer. The car windows were closed and the air conditioning system was on, but I could still hear the people praying — their prayers sounded like the buzzing of many bees.

I'd always wanted to see God move in revival, but the atmosphere in Korea convinced me that God would bring revival to my nation. This conviction stirred me to write the songs for an album called, *Awaken the Nations* and gave me a longing to see the church come alive. I wanted to see Christians strong in prayer and intercession, in praise and worship, in preaching the word and evangelism. I believe that today we're seeing a partial fulfilment of what I saw in Korea, but there's so much more to come. That time in Korea gave me a great passion to see praise and worship at the centre of church life and set me on a course to discover more of God's heart for worship.

My ministry has evolved from my spiritual pilgrimage. I've always had a wonderful sense of God's presence and have seen the way that he moves through music, songs and the playing of instruments. I'm convinced that God will use praise and worship to speak to the lost. David said, 'He put a new song in my mouth, a hymn of praise to our God. Many will see and fear and put their trust in the LORD' (Ps 40:3).

I'm trying to find out as much as I can about God's heart for worship because I believe that worship is right at the centre of his universe. The Bible is full of praise to God for his majesty, his glory, his might, his strength, his mercy and his compassion. Heaven is filled with people singing praises to the Lamb; angels and archangels giving glory; cherubim and seraphim crying, 'Holy, holy, holy is the Lord God Almighty'. And here on earth 'our chief end is,' as the Westminster Confession puts it, 'to glorify God and to enjoy him for ever'. God has taken me through many experiences and now I want him to use me to express his heart for his people and to help them to express their hearts to him.

a HEART
for REVIVAL

Revival — a time when God visits his people with manifestations of glory and power, a time when he purifies them, restores biblical truth and effects change in society. Church history abounds with revivals and one of the most recent in British history is the Welsh Revival of 1904. When God poured out his Holy Spirit in Wales, over 100,000 were swept into the kingdom in a two year period. Night after night chapels were filled with praying, worshipping people and meetings often lasted for hours on end.

The revival began in the village of Loughor which was then situated on the border between Glamorganshire and Carmarthanshire. The River Loughor flowed for a few miles near the coast and then opened up into a marvellous wide estuary. On one side of this estuary was the Carmarthanshire coast, and on the other was the beautiful Gower Peninsular with its picturesque bays — Rhossili, Oxwitch, Port Eynon, Caswell and the Mumbles. Loughor was known for its coal mines, steel works and foundries, so it was a significant place during the industrial revolution.

My mother grew up in Loughor. Her father was actually converted in the Welsh Revival and she lived with him, her mother and sister at an end-of-terrace cottage which was very near the Broad Oak coal mine. Up the road from their house was the River Loughor with its marshes and an enormous slag heap where the waste from the mine was deposited.

Every year, from the time that I was very small, my parents used to take my sister and me to Loughor for our annual summer holiday. It was always an exciting event. My father would plan the journey from Tongham in Surrey to Wales like a military operation. Then we'd squeeze into our small Austin 7 with our suitcases and our sandwiches and thermos flask of tea and we'd set off for what was then an incredible expedition which lasted around twelve hours.

My father would always plan the journey so that we could stop off at places like the Cheddar Caves, Gloucester Cathedral, or Birdlip Hill, a beauty spot near Gloucester. Of course, in those days there was no in-car entertainment, so we'd while away the time singing hymns and choruses as a family. My sister and I would often experiment with harmonies and always had great fun. Those trips became times of worship and times when our spiritual heritage was built into us. Once we arrived, we'd be packed into the end-of-terrace cottage where my mother spent her childhood.

The Broad Oak Mine was open during the first few years of my life. I used to watch the miners coming off their shift, with their lamps fixed to their pit helmets and coal dust all over their faces and clothes. Often they'd be singing.

It was during those holidays that I first heard about the revival. Even when I was very young, I was fascinated with the stories of crowds streaming to hear the word of God, packed chapels and thousands of conversions. I particularly loved to hear about Evan Roberts, who was a leading figure in the revival. He grew up in a little cottage called 'Island House', which was near the estuary marshes of the River Loughor, about 150 metres down the hill from where my mother grew up. When my mother was a little girl she would often play outside the Roberts' house and sit on Evan Roberts' knee. When he came back from various trips, he'd gather the children around him and give them all a penny each.

As I grew older my interest in the revival increased and I started asking questions about what happened. Steadily my own heart began longing for God to pour out his Spirit — not just in Wales but in the United Kingdom. When I was in my late teens, and just after I'd been baptised in the Spirit, my grandmother arranged for me to meet Evan Roberts' elderly sister, Sarah. Island House was neat and clean. I walked past a typical Welsh dresser and noticed some brown photographs on the sideboard. The family Bible was in evidence and there were texts on the wall. This was the place where Evan had grown up as a child.

Sarah Roberts' grey hair was tied back in a bun. I sat down with her and began to ask her as many questions as I could think of about Evan's character and zeal for God. 'What was his secret?' I asked. She pointed through the window to a shed in the back garden and explained that when he was a very young man he'd come home from the pit and immediately go there to pray. The miners didn't have the luxury of bathrooms in the cottages, so while Evan's mother prepared his bath tub in front of the fire, Evan — still covered with coal dust — would sit in the shed and pour out his heart to God. He'd spend hours there, developing his relationship with his heavenly Father and interceding for others.

In his day, the presence of the mine and steel works charged the social atmosphere. People worked hard, drank a lot and gambled. They also enjoyed singing. Evan was very interested in music and loved singing. He was also a gifted poet and was perhaps more artistically sensitive than many of the other lads with whom he grew up.

In his early teens he went to work in the Broad Oak Mine and began to develop a deep passion for God. He'd often stand at the pithead as the miners stepped into the cage that took them down to the mine and give them each a verse of scripture to meditate on. When they came up at the end of their shift he'd be there again, asking them what they'd thought about their particular scripture. Such was his zeal for God and for evangelism. The owner of the mine who ran the local school, noticed Evan and asked him to teach mathematics, music and morals in the school. By this time Evan was in his mid teens and God was forming his character and preparing him for revival.

As I sat there in that tiny cottage and heard the stories about Evan, I realised that God could use me too. I started longing for revival and began to pray, 'Do it again, Lord. Please do it again.'

The village of Loughor abounds in chapels. In several streets there's one every few yards and some of them hold hundreds of people. Between 1904 and 1906 these chapels were absolutely packed. The people who were caught up in the revival put a strong emphasis on worship. Sometimes whole congregations would spontaneously break out into singing and some people would sing extemporaneously under the anointing of the Spirit. Eifion Evans comments:

> 'The verse of the Welsh hymn "The man who suffered under the nails for a sinful man like me" was repeated several times. Many of the congregation, in the ecstasy of their spiritual deliverance, were unable to restrain

*themselves from dancing without either inhibition or
irreverence.'*

The Welsh Revival of 1904, Eifion Evans, Evangelical Press of Wales, 1974.

W.T. Stead, a London journalist came to Wales to report on
the revival. He noted that:

> '*Three quarters of the meeting consists of singing. No
> one uses a hymn book. No one gives out a hymn. The
> last person to control the meeting in any way is Mr
> Evan Roberts ... People pray and sing, give testimony;
> exhort as the Spirit moves them.'*

The Welsh Revival of 1904, Eifion Evans, Evangelical Press of Wales, 1974.

This outpouring of the Spirit recovered heartfelt, spontaneous
worship which had been lost in dry, formal, liturgical church
gatherings. Revival does this. Man lays his best plans and
God manifests himself in power and holiness and sweeps
them away in a torrent of irresistible blessing.

My interest in revival and my longing to see it stirred me to
find out what happened in worship in church history and
during times of revival. I discovered that many outpourings
of God's Holy Spirit had been accompanied by a new wave
of worship and music.

A GLANCE BACK AT WORSHIP

After the early church fathers died, the singing of psalms,
hymns and spiritual songs seemed to take a very low priority
in the life of the church. In fact, church history tells us very
little about how the early church worshipped. One reason for
this may hinge on the conversion of the Greeks who held a
view about music which has been called 'the doctrine of
ethos'. Their system of music was based on certain scales
called modes which they believed could affect character and

behaviour. They believed that man could be morally changed through the arts, particularly music and drama. Naturally, the Christians believed that only the gospel could affect moral change. So to make sure that there was no pagan influence on how the new converts regarded the use of music in worship, music was hardly used at all. So the church moved away from the psalms, hymns and spiritual songs that had characterised the gatherings of the first generation believers.

During the second century the gnostics and arians wrote hymns in which they put across their heretical teachings. In the third century Ephraim Cyrus, a distinguished father in the Syrian church, wrote hymns to counteract their heresy.

In the time of Constantine, Ambrose of Milan began to preach in Europe. He was a very charismatic preacher and his ministry was accompanied by signs, wonders, miracles and other gifts of the Spirit. He was very musical and wrote hymns so that the common people could worship God and latch onto his doctrine. In a famous history of music by Ebenezer Prout there's a picture of an engraving which depicts Ambrose of Milan baptising Augustine. There's a dove landing on Augustine and they're both singing. Prout says that the two men are 'spontaneously singing in a religious or spiritual ecstasy'. They were probably singing in the Spirit.

In the fifth century, Pope Gregory the Great (590-604) tried to 'purify' church music. The Gregorian chant was established and everyone had to sing in unison without musical instruments. This restriction was an attempt to keep Christian worship separate from secular art.

The Reformation in the sixteenth century not only affected the church's doctrine, it also renewed its worship. Luther himself was a skilled musician who could play both the lute and the flute. He declared:

> *'I really believe, nor am I shamed to assert, that next to theology there is no art equal to music ... Praising music is like trying to paint a great subject on a small canvas, which turns out merely a daub. But my love for it abounds; it has often refreshed me and freed me from great troubles.'*
>
> The Life and Letters of Martin Luther, New York: Barnes and Noble, Inc. 1911, 1968.
> Quoted in The Contemporary Music Debate by Steve Miller, Tyndale Publishers, Inc.
> Wheaton, Illinois, © 1993 by Steve Miller.

Luther's hymns and spiritual songs departed from the stylised art form of the Catholic church. His songs appealed to the common people because they were written in simple language and melody, and were very much in the style of the popular ballads of his day. In fact the troubadours and minstrels used to add his songs to their repertoire and go from town to town singing and playing them in the taverns. So Luther's songs became an integral part of German cultural life.

He didn't worry about the associations or origins of the tunes, so long as they were able to convey spiritual truth. In fact the words, 'Why should the devil have all the good music?' were probably first said not by William Booth, Larry Norman, or Cliff Richard, but by Martin Luther!

Luther established a whole new tradition of hymn singing in Germany. He believed that music could open hearts and set them ablaze, and he also realised that songs were vehicles for truth — as people sang them, they learnt the great doctrines of Scripture. We still sing some of his hymns today, the most popular being, 'A stronghold sure our God is still.' It's been said that Martin Luther did more damage to his enemies by his hymns than by his preaching.

When the Reformation was in full force in Geneva, John Calvin tried to break away from traditional Catholic church music. He believed that music used in worship should be biblical and encouraged the setting of psalms to music. These weren't always popular and were described in a rather derogatory way as 'Geneva Gigs'. Nevertheless, they still played a prominent part in the spiritual move of the reformation at that time.

The Puritan Revival in England was in the seventeenth century. The Puritans were more influenced by Geneva and the singing of psalms than they were by Luther and the singing of hymns. After the restoration of the monarchy during the time of King Charles II, the spiritual life of the nation began to decline. The established church lacked conviction and direction and many of the dissenting Puritans became too middle class and respectable.

Some people kept the fire of evangelical life alight. One of these was John Bunyan, who wrote *Pilgrim's Progress*. He wanted to see congregations singing spiritual songs and included many singable poetic passages in *Pilgrim's Progress*. By this time, the church was in such a poor state that his congregation became divided over the issue of hymn singing. Some people wanted to stick with the old metrical psalms, while others preferred to sing hymns with more popular tunes. Eventually, there was a division. Those who wanted to sing the hymns did so, while everyone else waited in the church lobby until they'd finished.

Isaac Watts was born in Southampton in 1674 and grew up in a good evangelical home. When he was a boy he was always writing verses and one day his father apparently said to him, 'Isaac why do you keep writing all this poetry? You will never grow up to be anything if all you do is write poetry.' But Isaac wouldn't stop. In desperation, his father declared, 'Isaac, if you don't stop writing this poetry I will have to give you a good thrashing.' Isaac's response was to leave a note which said,

Oh father, do some pity take
And I will no more verses make.

When Isaac Watts became a pastor, he was already gaining a reputation as a poet and soon began to express his evangelical beliefs in poetic form. In 1707 he published his hymns and spiritual songs in the first part of his *System of Praise*. The second part appeared in 1719.

By now, the metrical psalms that had originated in Geneva were making worship formal, boring and lifeless. Isaac broke away from them and began to write hymns on spiritual themes like wrath and mercy, original sin, justification by faith, election, sovereign and free grace, the shortness and misery of life and the gospel message. 'Behold the glories of the Lamb' is generally thought to be his first hymn. Benson says of Watts:

> *'He produced a whole cycle of religious song which his own ardent faith made devotional, which his manly and lucid mind made simple and strong, which his poetic feeling and craftsmanship made rhythmical and often lyrical, and which his sympathy with the people made hymnic.'*
>
> *The English Hymn*, Louis F. Benson, London, 1915.

So Isaac Watts was a great theologian, philosopher, mathematician and linguist — he learnt Latin, Hebrew and Greek. And he was an excellent poet. The traditional church considered his hymn writing to be in bad taste because it wasn't appropriate to use poetry to express spiritual truth. However, Isaac Watts gained the reputation of being the 'father of English hymns' and laid the foundation for the hymns and music of the next great move of God, which was the Wesleyan Revival.

The great eighteenth century Methodist Revival under Whitefield and Wesley produced many more great hymns. John and Charles Wesley both knew Isaac Watts and it's possible that the style of his hymns influenced Charles, whose output of over 6,000 hymns surpasses anyone before or after him. E. H. Broadbent notes two important aspects of this revival when he says:

> 'They contain in beautiful and arresting form sound expositions of many of the principle doctrines taught in scripture, and they express worship, and inward experiences of the Spirit in a way which make them continually suited to give utterance to the longings and praises of hearts touched by the Spirit of God.'
>
> *The Pilgrim Church*, E. H. Broadbent, Basingstoke, Pickering and Inglis, 1974.

So what John Wesley was preaching, his brother was putting into poetic doctrinal form. Charles wasn't afraid to combine the sacred and the secular. He set his hymns to the music that people were used to hearing in the inns and taverns, and borrowed melodies from folk songs, comic operas and oratorios. Because of this, he was often charged with being worldly, but his one concern was to communicate the biblical message.

Worship played a very significant part of this move of God. We still sing many of Charles Wesley's hymns today — although with far fewer verses than he originally wrote. Two of the most well known are: 'And can it be' and 'Hark, the herald angels sing'. Many of his hymns weren't based on objective truth, but on experience — particularly the ones about the Holy Spirit. For instance the hymn, 'Come Holy Ghost, all quickening fire' has seven verses. The first goes:

> Come, Holy Ghost, all-quickening fire,
> Come, and my hallowed heart inspire,

> *Sprinkled with the atoning blood:*
> *Now to my soul Thyself reveal;*
> *Thy mighty working let me feel,*
> *And know that I am born of God.*

Each verse builds on the previous one until we get to the last verse:

> *Come, Holy Ghost, all-quickening fire,*
> *My consecrated heart inspire,*
> *Sprinkled with the atoning blood:*
> *Still to my soul Thyself reveal;*
> *Thy mighty working may I feel,*
> *And know that I am one with God!*

Music played an important part in the Wesleys' evangelistic meetings. The words were clear, the tunes were popular and there were many songs that actually communicated the gospel message. It's said that the Methodist Revival became the most powerful evangelistic tool that England has ever known. Its hymns communicated the gospel and helped the people to understand their faith.

The next great move of God in England was in the nineteenth century. William Booth was a young Methodist minister who lived and worked in the East End of London. He held revival campaigns and saw many people saved. By that time, the fire of revival had died down and Methodism couldn't cope with the new influx of converts. So Booth founded the Salvation Army outside the *Blind Beggar Pub* in Whitechapel, East London. That was in 1865. Booth adopted the phrase, 'Why should the devil have all the good music?' and within a few years he was communicating the gospel through uniforms, brass bands and banners. Since brass bands were particularly popular in Victorian England, Booth used them to great effect.

William Booth was happy to put new words to songs from the music halls and theatres. So, 'Champagne Charlie is my name' became 'Bless his name, he sets me free'. And, 'Here's the good old whiskey. Mop it down, mop it down' became 'Storm the forts of darkness, bring them down, bring them down'. As the Army marched through the streets of England, it was often attacked and mobbed by the 'Skeleton Army' — a group of people financed by the brewers who were losing custom because of Booth's success in saving drunkards. The church criticised him but his Army changed the face of Victorian England and did a lot to bring about social reform in England. What's more, by the turn of the century, they'd taken the gospel to over eighty nations.

Other significant moves of God were accompanied by new music. The evangelistic campaigns of D. L. Moody were enriched by the music of Ira Sankey, a soloist who wrote songs in a well-liked style. At the time of these campaigns, the waltz was a popular contemporary dance and Sankey made full use of the lilting three/four rhythm for many of his hymns. A number of churches still sing songs like, 'Master, the tempest is raging' and 'Faith is the victory'.

A GLANCE AT WORSHIP TODAY

We have a rich heritage of evangelical Spirit-inspired music. Several years ago, Christians looked back at the New Testament church, noted its life, vitality, creativity, Spirit-led worship and body ministry, and realised that twentieth century church life was going through decline and neglect. Church music was becoming static and people were putting more emphasis on the artistic aspect than on the spiritual.

However, over the last twenty years the charismatic movement has released a great stream of psalms, hymns and spiritual songs into the church. There's been a renewal of praise and worship which has been pioneered by such song writers as Jimmy and Carol Owens, David and Dale Garrett, and Graham Kendrick. These writers, and others, are composing songs which reflect what God is doing among us, whatever our church background. We're singing similar songs at most major Christian events and are learning about how we can open our hearts more to God. Worship is also giving us a much greater sense of unity — when we're all praising God together, we tend to forget our theological differences.

God is restoring worship in his church, and the restoration of worship is always linked to something else — a mighty outpouring of the Holy Spirit. One of the significant things about the end time move of the Spirit in revival is this: God will have a people of praise throughout the nations. Two popular worship songs were written in the '70s:

For I'm building a people of power
And I'm making a people of praise,
That will move through this land by my Spirit,
And will glorify my precious name.

All over the world the Spirit is moving,
All over the world as the prophet said it would be;
All over the world, there's a mighty revelation
Of the glory of the Lord, as the waters cover the sea.

When these two songs were written, they were looking forward to a time when God's Spirit would be moving right across the earth. Today there's a much greater fulfilment of what those songs were pointing towards.

The worship songbook of the early church was the book of Psalms and this speaks again and again of the glory of God in the nations and of a people of praise.

'Sing praises to the LORD, enthroned in Zion; proclaim among the nations what he has done' (Ps 9:11).

'The earth is the LORD's, and everything in it, the world, and all who live in it' (Ps 24:1).

'Let your sharp arrows pierce the hearts of the king's enemies; let the nations fall beneath your feet. Your throne, O God, will last for ever and ever; a sceptre of justice will be the sceptre of your kingdom ... I will perpetuate your memory through all generations; therefore the nations will praise you for ever and ever' (Ps 45:5,6,17).

'I will be exalted among the nations, I will be exalted in the earth' (Ps 46:10).

'Clap your hands, all you nations ... For God is the King of all the earth; sing to him a psalm of praise. God reigns over the nations; God is seated on his holy throne. The nobles of the nations assemble as the people of the God of Abraham, for the kings of the earth belong to God; he is greatly exalted' (Ps 47:1,7–9).

'May God be gracious to us and bless us and make his face shine upon us, that your ways may be known on earth, your salvation among all nations. May the peoples praise you, O God; may all the peoples praise you. May the nations be glad and sing for joy, for you rule the peoples justly and guide the nations of the earth. May the peoples praise you, O God; may all the peoples praise you. Then the land will yield its harvest *(that's revival), and God, our God, will bless us. God will bless us, and all the ends of the earth will fear him'* (Ps 67).

Isaiah once brought a great Messianic prophecy about the coming of the Lord Jesus and the establishment of his kingdom. In it, God promised to bring righteousness and praise into every nation.

'I delight greatly in the LORD; my soul rejoices in my God. For he has clothed me with garments of salvation and arrayed me in a robe of righteousness, as a bridegroom adorns his head like a priest, and as a bride adorns herself with her jewels. For as the soil makes the young plant come up and a garden causes seeds to grow, so the Sovereign LORD will make righteousness and praise spring up before all nations' (Is 61:10–11).

Never before has there been such a release of praise and worship throughout the earth. Never before has the church seen believers in every nation singing and listening to Christian music, and praising God together as they are now. Could this restoration of worship be heralding a mighty outpouring of the Spirit that ushers in the return of Jesus? 'Do it again, Lord. Please do it again.'

CHAPTER 3

I am DOING

a NEW THING

When Rosie and I were on holiday in North Africa we decided to drive down to the Sahara Desert. It was perhaps not the most inspiring place for a break, but it held sufficient interest value for us to make the trip. We drove into the foothills of the Atlas mountains and made the steady climb round various hairpin bends.

It was early summer and the winter snows still covering the highest peaks were beginning to melt and form streams which ran down the side of the mountain. The friends who were with us told us that once we got over the other side, we'd be on the edge of the Sahara. Sure enough, the landscape soon became barren and sandy — just as you'd expect in a desert.

We travelled along the hot dusty road for many miles. Then we stopped, got out of the car and looked down into a deep gorge. It was one of the most amazing sights I've ever seen. In this parched, sandy, dry place was a band of green about a mile wide running right through the desert. It was a river. Coming off it were irrigation channels which watered fields where crops were growing. Beside it there were threshing floors and little villages. And along its banks there were giant palm trees. The noise made by the breeze blowing through these palms sounded like the clapping of giant hands. I recalled Isaiah's words, 'all the trees of the field will clap their hands' (Is 55:12).

The river reminded me of the many passages of scripture which speak about the river of God. It's there in the beginning. Genesis 2:10 says:

> *'A river watering the garden flowed from Eden.'*

And it's there at the end. Revelation 22:1–2 says:

> *'Then the angel showed me the river of the water of life, as clear as crystal, flowing from the throne of God and of the Lamb down the middle of the great street of the city. On each side of the river stood the tree of life, bearing twelve crops of fruit, yielding its fruit every month. And the leaves of the tree are for the healing of the nations.'*

During this trip we were reminded of all kinds of biblical imagery to do with water. We drove for miles from a Sahara village across the sand dunes and suddenly found a pool in the middle of the desert. It was very beautiful. There were flamingos on the pool and around its edge were little bushes and plants. In another place we saw a geyser. Rivers, pools, streams — all these are biblical images which speak about the power and presence of the Holy Spirit making the barren fruitful.

Several of the Old Testament prophets refer to the river of God. Isaiah says:

'The desert and the parched land will be glad; the wilderness will rejoice and blossom. Like the crocus, it will burst into bloom; it will rejoice greatly and shout for joy. The glory of Lebanon will be given to it, the splendour of Carmel and Sharon; they will see the glory of the LORD, the splendour of our God ... Water will gush forth in the wilderness and streams in the desert. The burning sand will become a pool, the thirsty ground bubbling springs. In the haunts where jackals once lay, grass and reeds and papyrus will grow. And a highway will be there; it will be called the Way of Holiness' (Is 35:1–2, 6–8).

Ezekiel spoke prophetically about the river of God, and it was this passage which stuck with me as we made our way through the Sahara.

'The man brought me back to the entrance of the temple, and I saw water coming out from under the threshold of the temple towards the east (for the temple faced east). The water was coming down from under the south side of the temple, south of the altar. He then brought me out through the north gate and led me round the outside to the outer gate facing east, and the water was flowing from the south side.

'As the man went eastward with a measuring line in his hand, he measured off a thousand cubits and then led me through water that was ankle-deep. He measured off another thousand cubits and led me through water that was knee-deep. He measured off another thousand and led me through water that was up to the waist. He measured off another thousand, but now it was a river that I could not cross, because the water had risen and was deep enough to swim in — a river that no-one could cross. He asked me, "Son of man, do you see this?"

> *'Then he led me back to the bank of the river. When I arrived there, I saw a great number of trees on each side of the river. He said to me, "This water flows towards the eastern region and goes down into the Arabah, where it enters the Sea. When it empties into the Sea, the water there becomes fresh. Swarms of living creatures will live wherever the river flows. There will be large numbers of fish, because this water flows there and makes the salt water fresh; so where the water flows everything will live"' (Ezek 47:1–9).*

I was prompted to pray and to see if the river imagery was consistent in Scripture. The key seemed to be 'where the water flows everything will live'. Ezekiel's prophecy goes on to talk about fishermen becoming catchers of fish and about all kinds of fruit trees growing along the banks of the river. The leaves of these trees won't wither and, like the tree of life in Revelation, their fruit will serve for food and their leaves for healing. It's a graphic picture of the Holy Spirit bringing refreshment to the church and nation.

In Jesus' time the Feast of Pentecost gave thanks for the early rain which produced the harvest, and the Feast of Tabernacles gave thanks for the final harvest. The last and greatest day of the Feast of Tabernacles was a very joyful occasion. The priests would be there with their trumpets, the people would wave their palms and there would be tremendous rejoicing. The high priest would take a pitcher of water from the Pool of Siloam through the Water Gate and into the temple, where he'd pour the water over the altar. That water was a symbol of the rain that brought fruitfulness and caused the harvest to grow.

In the context of this solemn occasion Jesus stood up and interrupted the proceedings — something for which he could have been arrested. We read, 'Jesus stood and said in a loud voice, "If anyone is thirsty, let him come to me and drink. Whoever believes in me, as the Scripture has said, streams of living water will flow from within him'" (John 7:37). Jesus was linking the images of water, river and rain with the power and the presence of the Holy Spirit who would come after he'd defeated Satan at the cross, risen from the dead and ascended into heaven. When we look at Old Testament scriptures about the river of God, streams in the desert, pools and rains, we're seeing a picture of the Spirit making the church fruitful.

I was particularly stirred by the river in the desert theme because it coincided with a powerful and unusual outpouring of the Spirit in Church of Christ the King (CCK), Brighton. This outpouring was particularly prevalent in Toronto, Canada and was touching many churches in the UK and throughout the world. I'd always wanted God to move in revival power, and now I had a rising expectation that he was going to pour out his Spirit on his church and affect the nation.

When I was in Korea in 1991, I experienced revival phenomena first hand. On my return something happened which had a dramatic effect on me. It was as though I was given a 'spirit of prayer' for several days and couldn't sleep. During that time I'd often get up in the early hours of the morning, walk round Preston Park and cry out to God for revival.

One night I was in the park when I had an awesome experience of the presence of God. Through my mind appeared a video re-run of things I'd done that I regretted and people I'd hurt. I was gripped by a terrible fear of judgement and had the sense that God would kill me. I felt totally undone and unworthy to be in his presence. Then suddenly, superimposed on this video picture was a vision of the cross and the Father seemed to be saying to me, 'Don't

49

worry son. It's all right. You're forgiven. It's all washed away. You're free from this.' I felt such relief and joy that the blood of Jesus had cleansed every sin.

This was a turning point in my spiritual history because it intensified my desire to see revival, stirred me to seek God in a new way and began to affect the songs that I was writing. I wrote the words of the song, 'Let your word run freely through this nation' at this time and my son, Nathan, wrote the tune. The song reflects the revival theme:

> *Let your word run freely through this nation*
> *Strong Deliverer break the grip of Satan's power*
> *Let the cross of Jesus shine above the idols of this land*
> *Let anointed lives rise up and take their stand.*

I soon discovered that God was speaking about revival to several of my fellow elders who shared my increasing expectation that God was going to pour out his Spirit. This awareness of impending revival started to affect my preaching and worship leading. It also affected our worship team who began to realise the importance of worship in revival. We all recognised the sovereignty of God — that he won't break in because of who we are or what we do. But we also knew that in his sovereignty he was stirring us to pray. As Matthew Henry, the great Puritan commentator said, 'Before God is going to do any great work he sets his people a-praying.'

In the autumn of 1993 there was a much greater level of expectation in our worship times at CCK. One evening, we were singing about the power of God when the lead guitarist, under the inspiration of the Holy Spirit, began to play very aggressively, illustrating musically what we were singing about. Suddenly a spirit of prophecy came upon some of the church leaders and people began to come forward for prayer. The Spirit was falling on them powerfully. Some were shaking, others experienced a wonderful sense of God's peace and several sank to the floor.

One of our elders, Alan Preston, was preaching one Sunday morning. Towards the end of his message he invited people to come and kneel at the front, which many of them did. Around this time God was highlighting the theme of consecration, drawing us into deeper fellowship with him. One of the songs that we were singing quite a lot was, 'Anointing, fall on me' with its cry to God, 'Touch my hands, my mouth and my heart. Fill my life, Lord, every part.'

In February 1994 a young man gave a powerful prophecy at a Saturday morning prayer meeting. In essence it was, 'Prepare for disruption'. The elders weighed the word carefully, with the result that the church was called together to pray about it the following Sunday night. The church leaders were thrilled to see about six hundred people turn up. By now, the whole church sensed that we were on the edge of a great visitation from God.

Gradually, reports of a move of God's Spirit in Toronto filtered through to us. Alan Preston went to Toronto and met with God in a very powerful way. On his first Sunday back, God disrupted us. During worship, his presence was so strong that people were shaking and falling down. The church had to learn quickly how to minister in this kind of situation.

God's visitation really challenged the worship team and me, because we were right in the forefront of it all. Things often happened during worship and we had to adjust our programme to make room for the Spirit. For a while we found that dynamic warlike songs weren't necessarily appropriate for what God was doing. We also found that this visitation was challenging our ideas of structure and form in worship. Occasionally we'd arrive with our songlist and discover that we wouldn't need it, or we'd find that a prophetic word would change the course of a meeting.

God's Spirit even challenged the time that we gave to preaching. Both leaders and people highly valued the exposition of God's word and saw it as an integral part of the worship time. But we knew that when God stepped in, we had to make room for him to move.

We began to hold 'River of God' meetings — times when we could worship, receive a small amount of teaching and, above all, drink more from God. These meetings were frequently interrupted with outbursts of laughter as the Holy Spirit came on people. Sometimes demons manifested themselves and made a noise. We had to deal with that — setting individuals free as lovingly and sensitively as we could. People often did strange things. They'd shake, jerk or lie prostrate on the floor. It was hard to explain everything that was happening, but we knew that God was with us.

This new move of the Spirit profoundly affected me and my worship ministry. The experience I had when I returned from Korea was one of many personal visitations from God. A few months before the new move of the Spirit began, I was sitting worshipping at the piano at home, when the presence of Jesus came into the room in the same way as it had come when I was a boy (only this time there was no canary).

One morning I met Alan in his office. He'd recently got back from Toronto and I wanted to hear what had happened. He shared some of his experiences and asked me to pray for him. I said that he should be praying for me. We ended up praying for each other, experiencing the power of God and falling on the floor. Some time later we learnt that the Spirit had also come on the church receptionist who was sitting at her usual place outside the room.

The move of the Spirit was affecting the content of our worship times. We began singing new songs which invited the Spirit to come, praised God for what was happening and gave a prophetic interpretation. We were provoked by songs about rivers, rain, wind, and the breath of God. Paul Oakley, one of our songwriters, wrote a song called, 'Let it rain' which he was going to teach to the congregation one Sunday morning.

On Sundays the worship band usually practise from 8.30am to 9.30am and then have half an hour's break before the main meeting starts. But that morning the presence of God fell on them while they were rehearsing Paul's song and they just kept worshipping. As people came in, they caught what was happening and joined in. Everyone was still singing the song well after 10.00am and many individuals were experiencing manifestations of the presence of God. The rain was certainly falling.

John Wilthew was one of our elders before we sent him out to become lead elder of another church. Several weeks before he left, he was at one of our Saturday morning prayer meetings. The next day he was going to preach on fanning into flame the gift of God (2 Tim 1:6) so a few of us gathered round him to pray for him. While we were praying, a young man walked up and said, 'I have a prophetic word for you — ruach'. The Holy Spirit immediately fell on John who remained sprawled over his chair in a state of stupor for the rest of the meeting.

I left the meeting thinking about this word, ruach, which refers to the 'wind of God' and when I got home I wrote a song about it. That evening, one of the members of the worship team was celebrating his fortieth birthday. At his party several of us were talking about the move of the Spirit and I told one of the people there what had happened at the prayer meeting. Immediately I said the word, ruach, the Spirit of God came on him and he fell over. The next morning I taught the song and John preached. John was still under the influence of the Spirit and had to cling to the pulpit for support. His speech was slightly slurred, but he spoke powerfully. It was a memorable time.

Soon after this we decided to hold a series of nightly 'River of God' meetings. Before each meeting the worship team got together to pray. One evening we were praying and I fell on the floor. I wasn't experiencing anything extraordinary, but I couldn't get up — and I was supposed to be leading the worship in the meeting.

The prayer room emptied and the next thing I heard was Stuart Townend's voice leading the congregation in the main hall on the floor above me. I was thinking, 'I'm supposed to be up there leading the worship, but I can't move.' Then I said, 'Lord, I don't want to go up there without your presence.' He replied, 'Why not? You've done that before.' His comment was awesome and frightening, but it also came with great grace. I had a wonderful sense of his peace and presence as I got up and rejoined the worship team.

That experience made me take worship leading even more seriously than I had before. I hadn't realised that I was depending more on my gift and experience than on the anointing of the Holy Spirit. Now I'm spending far more time preparing before the meetings.

Stoneleigh Bible Week a little later was a tremendous occasion because God just came and poured out his Spirit on us. I was responsible for leading the worship. Even though I've done this many times all around the world, standing in front of thousands of people can still be a very nerve-racking experience and you're totally dependent on God. But this Stoneleigh was different. It seemed as though God took all the pressure away. Of course, the singers and musicians worked hard on the songs and in their spiritual preparation. But it felt, in the words of Terry Virgo, as though God were inviting us to his meetings rather than our inviting him to ours.

This move of the Spirit is particularly challenging people who are involved in the worship ministry. It's bringing the challenges of holiness, anointing, sensitivity and prophetic awareness. It's affecting the kind of songs that we're writing. Many of the new songs are giving more space for instruments to play between verses because that's often the time when God moves in. We're learning how to avoid prejudging what's going to happen in the meetings and how to balance good preparation against the spontaneity of God. It's an exciting and exhilarating season and I'm praying that what we're enjoying in the church will spill over into the world.

This time of outpouring is also a time of preparation. Elisha called for a harpist and prophesied while the musician played. His prophecy was:

'"Make this valley full of ditches. For this is what the LORD says: You will see neither wind nor rain, yet this valley will be filled with water, and you, your cattle and your other animals will drink. This is an easy thing in the eyes of the LORD; he will also hand Moab over to you. You will overthrow every fortified city and every major town. You will cut down every good tree, stop up all the springs, and ruin every good field with stones." The next morning, about the time for offering the sacrifice, there it was — water flowing from the*

55

*direction of Edom! And the land was filled with water'
(2 Kings 3:16–20).*

The musician played, the hand of God came on the prophet and the land was filled with the presence of God. That's a picture of revival. There's worship, God's hand comes on the church and the land is filled with his glory.

Over the years we've discovered many lost truths through biblical preaching. Now worship is playing a very significant part. It's preparing people's hearts for God's presence and bringing unity to the church through songs which focus on truth and experiences of God. Church history bears witness to the fact that at times of revival there's a new flow of Spirit-inspired worship.

There are implications for everyone — worshippers, worship musicians, worship leaders and church leaders alike. We must all seek the presence of God — particularly if we're involved in worship ministry. One of our greatest desires should be this: that God's presence among us should become so intense that it might overflow into revival. We should also develop our technical ability to the point where we're no longer distracted by the mechanics of worship leading, but are worshipping God and sensing the move of his Spirit.

We need to be ready for revival. When the cloud of glory came down on the completed Temple, the priests couldn't minister. They'd been trained in Temple service. They'd learnt to prophesy, play instruments, sing psalms and submit to leadership. They were familiar with the structure of worship. But when God came, these things were peripheral — merely the scaffolding around God's manifestation of himself.

We must learn the disciplines of worship. Worship teams must know how to work together, play new songs and develop a sense of togetherness. And congregations must know how to participate in the meetings and be open to God. Our preparation isn't an end in itself. It's preparing us for an outpouring of the Spirit in us as individuals, in our churches and in our nation. When God comes, he'll bring his own agenda and we, like the Temple priests, may find ourselves unable to do anything except bow in wonder and awe.

in SPIRIT *and in* TRUTH

To the casual onlooker, the sparkling blue of the Aegean would have appeared inviting. To me, the sight of land was a relief. I'd been cruising around some of the Greek islands on a small boat on a less than peaceful sea. The islands were beautiful, the trip unforgettable. But as we approached the harbour of Piraeus, I suddenly forgot about my slight queasiness and allowed my imagination to travel back 2,000 years.

The temples on the hillside, though now in ruins, were the same temples that Paul would have seen when he sailed into Piraeus. As we passed them, my romantic dreaming turned to thoughts of what Paul did when he arrived in Athens. Standing on Mars Hill, he challenged the whole of Athens' cultural and religious life. An altar to an unknown God gave him the introduction he needed to preach about Jesus. He began by identifying a basic need in man — the need to worship. The evidence for this need was scattered all over the hills of Greece — the Greeks and their neighbours considered that the worship of various gods was an essential part of life.

Originally, God gave mankind a capacity for worship. But man rebelled and tried to fill that vacuum with anything other than God himself. Rather than worship the living God, man chose not to acknowledge or give thanks to him — with disastrous consequences.

> 'For although they knew God, they neither glorified him as God nor gave thanks to him, but their thinking became futile and their foolish hearts were darkened. Although they claimed to be wise, they became fools and exchanged the glory of the immortal God for images made to look like mortal man and birds and animals and reptiles' (Rom 1:21–23).

There's a basic awareness in man which tells him that he needs to find identity in something beyond himself. Primitive peoples, who were dependent on the elements for their livelihood, worshipped the sun, moon, wind and rain. They made idols which identified and personified these various powers and expressed their commitment to them through rituals, ceremonies and sacrifices of appeasement. Great civilisations were build up around their deities.

The Greeks and Romans worshipped gods and named such planets as Jupiter, Mercury and Mars after them. The Romans made Caesar into a god, while the early Philistines worshipped an idol called Dagon. When the Israelites were in the Promised Land, they were continually tempted to worship Baal. In Lystra, Paul and Barnabas were hailed as messengers of Mercury and in Ephesus, the gospel created a violent reaction among those whose commercial interests were bound up with the goddess Artemis. From the Aztecs to the Aborigines, from the Britons to the Babylonians, the worship of some form of deity was a normal part of life.

The idols that personified these gods had no power. The psalmist, in mocking tone, compares them with the God of Israel:

'The idols of the nations are silver and gold, made by the hands of men. They have mouths, but cannot speak, eyes, but they cannot see; they have ears, but cannot hear, nor is there breath in their mouths. Those who make them will be like them, and so will all who trust in them' (Ps 135:15–18).

Although the idols had no power in themselves, the priests, witch-doctors and other cultic leaders did have authority. They manipulated their gullible and fearful followers and drew on occult powers, often with dreadful and awesome manifestations. By their black arts, the magicians of Egypt were able to copy at least some of Moses' miracles. The ability to use psychic powers, to commune with departed spirits, to place curses and even heal the sick, were all connected with idol worship. Idolatry touched the invisible world.

Western man may not make idols to worship, but his rebellion against God remains. His spiritual vacuum still needs to be filled, so whether consciously or unconsciously, he can't help being a worshipper. The humanist turns man into a god. His ideas have penetrated education and politics, undermining godly values and making Christian values relevant only if they don't contradict his own. Today, the gods of materialism, pleasure, sex and the occult all vie for man's attention.

Man was made for a relationship with God, and God wants to receive his worship. In the Old Testament, God revealed himself most powerfully on Mount Sinai. Lightning flashed, thunder rumbled and God revealed his righteous laws by which the human race was to live. His first two commandments challenged every man-made idea of God and every obscure form of worship:

'You shall have no other gods before me. You shall not make for yourself an idol in the form of anything in heaven above or on the earth beneath or in the waters below. You shall not bow down to them or worship them; for I, the LORD your God, am a jealous God, punishing the children for the sin of the fathers to the third and fourth generation of those who hate me, but showing love to a thousand generations of those who love me and keep my commandments' (Ex 20:3–6).

God's special instructions to the Israelites set them apart as a nation through whom he'd reveal himself to mankind. This revelation would culminate in the birth of the Messiah.

The journey from Egypt to Canaan should have taken only eleven days, but the Israelites disobeyed, grumbled and rebelled, so it took them forty years. On the edge of the promised land, Moses addressed them, recalling all that God had said and done for them, and bringing his final exhortations and warnings. The book of Deuteronomy records Moses' words and gives the conditions of God's blessing in the promised land. If the people obeyed, God would bless them; if they disobeyed, he would curse them. Moses reminded them of their uniqueness as a people and warned them to live apart from the influences and idolatry of other nations.

Along with the promise of a land flowing with milk and honey came the charge, 'Hear, O Israel: The LORD our God, the LORD is one. Love the LORD your God with all your heart and with all your soul and with all your strength' (Deut 6:4–5). God didn't want his people to be slaves to the rigors of an impossible law. He wanted them to obey him out of a loving relationship.

Love is at the heart of the law and it's expressed in obedience. A heart relationship with God couldn't involve idolatry any more than murder, covetousness, lying and adultery. The tragedy of Israel's backslidings was this: her love for God grew cold. The inevitable results were rebellion and idolatry.

The Old Covenant provided God's law, but his people couldn't keep it. God's master plan gradually unfolded as the prophets proclaimed a time when a New Covenant would replace the old. This Covenant would be based on a new relationship, as Jeremiah prophesied:

> '"The time is coming," declares the LORD, "when I will make a new covenant with the house of Israel and with the house of Judah. It will not be like the covenant I made with their forefathers when I took them by the hand to lead them out of Egypt, because they broke my covenant, though I was a husband to them," declares the LORD. "This is the covenant that I will make with the house of Israel after that time," declares the LORD. "I will put my law in their minds and write it on their hearts. I will be their God, and they will be my people"' (Jer 31:31–33).

Commenting on this prophecy, the writer to the Hebrews sheds light on the nature of this New Covenant. He explains that the first covenant had rules and regulations which governed the practice of divine worship at the Tabernacle. The priests ministered on behalf of the people using various objects such as a golden altar, a golden lampstand and the ark of the covenant. The weakness of this form of worship was this: it was 'not able to clear the conscience' because it was related to outward form (Heb 9:9).

If people were going to obey God and love him from their hearts, they'd need a New Covenant which would give him the ability to respond to God in a loving way. This New Covenant would have to be mediated by someone who could reconcile a holy God to a sinful human race. Jesus perfectly fulfilled every aspect of Old Covenant life, so he was able to mediate the New Covenant. If God accepted Old Covenant rituals as a means of making people outwardly clean, 'How much more, then, will the blood of Christ, who through the eternal Spirit offered himself unblemished to God, cleanse our consciences from acts that lead to death, so that we may serve the living God!' (Heb 9:14)

Jesus made it possible for us to love God with our whole heart. His earthly life spoke of a loving relationship with his Father. His many confrontations with the legalistic Pharisees highlighted the stark contrast between a life dominated by rules and regulations and a life set free to enjoy a relationship with God. During a time of interrogation by the Pharisees, a lawyer tested Jesus with a question: 'Teacher, which is the greatest commandment in the Law?' Jesus' reply put in a nutshell the nature of New Covenant life.

> '"Love the Lord your God with all your heart and with all your soul and with all your mind. This is the first and greatest commandment." And the second is like it: "Love your neighbour as yourself." All the Law and the Prophets hang on these two commandments' (Mt 22:36–40).

The true nature of worship

In the time of Jesus, the Jews and Samaritans didn't get along too well — which is why the Samaritan woman was so astounded when Jesus asked her for a drink. When Jesus put his finger on an area of personal need in her life, she realised that he was a prophet and began to engage him in a religious discussion. We don't know whether she asked her questions out of curiosity or genuine interest, but we do know that Jesus' answers tell us what worship is really all about.

Worship isn't limited to a place

The woman wanted to know where people should go to worship God. At that time the Samaritans and Jews both followed the Law of Moses, but disagreed about where to worship. The Samaritans said that true worship should take place on Mount Gerizim near Shechem whereas the Jews favoured Mount Zion in Jerusalem. There was a certain amount of logic in both arguments. God had revealed himself to Moses on Mount Gerizim, but he'd spoken a bit later about worship on Mount Zion. So there was tension between the two nations.

The focus on a place for worship was an Old Covenant idea. When Jesus told the woman, 'It isn't important where you worship', he was pointing to a New Covenant arrangement which superseded the Old. Sometimes we can get sentimental about places. Maybe we remember the building where our church first started, or where God met with us powerfully. We must be careful not to build a shrine to it. Rather, we must remember that we can worship God anywhere.

Worship isn't based on tradition

The Samaritan woman commented, 'Our fathers worshipped on this mountain' (Jn 4:20). Jesus had to point out that it wasn't important what happened in the past because God was doing something new. It's very easy to start up a worship tradition and to end up being bound by it. We think, 'We start with three praise songs — all linked by a particular key, then someone reads a scripture, we have a tongue and an interpretation, a prophecy, a quieter song, a bit of singing in the Spirit and another quiet song.' We mustn't get locked into this kind of thing because God wants us to worship him in fresh creative ways. We must pray about this and be open to the new things that the Spirit is doing.

Worship comes from knowing God

Jesus told the woman, 'You Samaritans worship what you do not know' (Jn 4:22). Worship is for God, so it needs to be related to who he is. If we try to work out our own ideas of what God is like, we'll be worshipping what we don't know. But if we understand his character, we'll worship him as he wants us to. The more we know God, the more we'll want to worship him. God has revealed himself through creation and our consciences, but the clearest revelation of all comes through the Bible.

The Bible describes God as loving, righteous, holy, patient, full of goodness, just, wrathful and yet merciful. He's complete in himself — all powerful, all knowing and present everywhere. His names represent different aspects of his character:

El Elyon	*God most high*
El Olam	*the everlasting God*
El Shaddai	*God almighty*
El Elohim	*God of creation and providence*

The most common name for God is 'Yahweh' or 'Jehovah'. This name expresses his self-existence and his eternal unchangeable character. There are also several covenant names:

Jehovah Jireh	*the Lord my provider*
Jehovah Nissi	*the Lord my banner*
Jehovah Tsiadkeni	*the Lord my righteousness*
Jehovah Shalom	*the Lord my peace*
Jehovah Rapha	*the Lord my healer*
Jehovah Ra-ah	*the Lord my shepherd*

Whenever God dealt with people in the Old Testament, he acted consistently with his character. When we praise the Lord, we should remember his character as it's expressed in his different names.

Jesus tells us, 'the true worshippers will worship the Father' (Jn 4:23). To worship God as Father implies a relationship based on love. We enter this relationship through knowing and identifying with Jesus. The Father's special relationship with Jesus becomes ours the moment that we are in Christ. Through his death, Jesus reconciles us to God and gives us a new nature. God writes his laws on our hearts and pours out his love into our hearts by the Holy Spirit (Rom 5:5). No longer do we try to please him by our performance, we respond to his fatherhood. Our chief preoccupation is now to fulfil the greatest commandment — to love him with all our heart, soul, mind and strength. That was God's original intention — a harmonious relationship between himself and his people.

The Father seeks worshippers

We often get preoccupied with the sound of our worship. We worry about whether the songs were in the right key or whether we sang them too many times. But the Father isn't after good music. He's not so much concerned with the sound we make, but with our hearts. He's looking for worshippers who will worship him 'in spirit and truth' (Jn 4:23).

We need to understand these two dimensions. What's the place of the Spirit and the word in worship? Sometimes I hear people say, 'If only we could have longer times of worship without preaching'. But according to the Scriptures, preaching is worship. Paul says, 'Be filled with the Spirit. Speak to one another with psalms, hymns and spiritual songs. Sing and make music in your hearts to the Lord' (Eph 5:18–19). In this case, the Spirit produces worship. But then we read, 'Let the word of Christ dwell in you richly as you teach and admonish one another with all wisdom, and as you sing psalms, hymns and spiritual songs with gratitude in your hearts to God' (Col 3:16). Here the word produces worship. So New Testament worship is always in Spirit and truth.

The Spirit in worship

The natural result of the Spirit-filled life is worship. When the apostles were baptised in the Spirit on the Day of Pentecost, they spoke in tongues and glorified God. Tongues releases your heart to worship and helps you to express your deepest feelings to God.

The Greek word translated, 'worship' in John 4 is *proskuneo*, which means to come towards to kiss. This implies great intimacy. When Paul says, 'We ... are the circumcision, we who worship by the Spirit of God, who glory in Christ Jesus, and put no confidence in the flesh' (Phil 3:3), he uses the word, *latreuo*. This word has nothing to do with expressing intimacy. Rather it's about worshipping God in everything that we do. So we need the help of the Spirit to express intimacy with God in our worship times, and in the way we live with others.

The baptism in the Spirit isn't the same as being filled with the Spirit (Eph 5:18). When Paul says, 'be filled with the Spirit, he doesn't mean be filled in the same way as an empty glass is filled from a jug. He means, 'Be preoccupied with the Spirit' — just as you can be totally immersed in a hobby. God wants us to live each day under the control of the Spirit, so that when we come to a worship time, we'll be able to enjoy his presence right away. So true worship, which takes place in the realm of the Spirit, expresses intimacy and also embraces the whole realm of life's activities.

The word in worship

The word is also important in worship. We must be careful not to emphasise subjectivity, experiences and feelings. God's truth remains constant and it will sustain us when we're battling with emotions, pressures and trials. If we're going to be worshippers in truth, we must get truth into us. So let's study theology and read books like *The Knowledge of the Holy* by A. W. Tozer. Let's read and memorise scriptures about God's greatness — his faithfulness, mercy, justice, compassion and righteousness. Let's go through the psalms and learn what David said about God. Let's sing hymns that give us a sense of God-consciousness, which say things about God that are revealed in the Scriptures — hymns like:

> *Immortal, invisible, God only wise,*
> *In light inaccessible, hid from our eyes,*
> *Most blessed, most glorious, the Ancient of Days,*
> *Almighty, victorious, thy great name we praise.*
>
> Walter Chalmers Smith

If we know the word, we won't always be frantically leafing through the Bible to find a verse. The Scriptures will pour out of us and our worship will always have content.

The power of the word

The word has amazing power. On one occasion I was preaching on God's 'incomparably great power for us who believe' (Eph 1:19). I looked at God's intrinsic power — the fact that he's powerful, God's saving power — the fact that he's saved us from sin and the devil, and God's manifest power — the fact that he loves to manifest his presence among his people. When I finished preaching I was about to invite people forward for prayer when a lady interrupted me. She came to the front waving her hand in my face and saying,

'Look at this! Look at this!' She was being a bit disruptive, but was obviously in a state of great excitement so I said, 'Tell me what's happened'.

She replied, 'Twenty years ago I badly injured my wrist in an industrial accident at work. I had an operation, but it went tragically wrong. The surgeon severed the tendons between my wrist and my hand, which meant that from then on, my hand was clenched in a fist. I won a lot of industrial compensation for this. While you were preaching about the power of God, I believed that he could open my hand and the next thing I knew was that my thumb and two fingers were straight.'

By now she was incredibly excited — and so was I. Faith began rising in my heart and I commanded the other two fingers to move. I watched, awe-struck, as her whole palm became visible for the first time in twenty years. Later that week I had a letter from the minister of her church. He told me that she'd been opening and closing her hand all week and telling her neighbours what had happened. She'd also had the miracle medically verified. God had put back something that wasn't there. It was remarkable — one of the greatest miracles I've ever seen.

A few years ago there was a student called Zena in my local church. She was a lively young woman, then one day her leg almost became paralysed. She went to the doctor who performed various tests, but he couldn't explain the illness. He didn't know if it was a muscular problem or some form of virus, but he thought that it might help if she had her leg in plaster. When the plaster was removed, there was absolutely no change. There was no strength in her leg and she had to walk around on crutches. She returned to the hospital for more tests and I prayed for her, but there was no improvement.

After a little while, she asked me to pray for her again. I was reluctant because I'd prayed before — with no result. But she persisted and I relented. So one afternoon she came to my house with her home group leader. I had very little faith, but as we started to pray, God began to speak to me from the story of Abraham and Sarah. I recalled that 'By faith Abraham, even though he was past age — and Sarah herself was barren — was enabled to become a father because he considered him faithful who had made the promise' (Heb 11:11). What particularly struck me was the faithfulness of God, so I said to Zena, 'We're going to consider God's faithfulness.' We sang songs like, 'The steadfast love of the Lord never ceases' and looked up several scriptures about God's faithfulness and meditated on them. God's faithfulness was the centre of our attention. While we were worshipping and praying like this, Zena suddenly pushed aside her crutches and ran around the room, out of the room, up and down the stairs and into the street. God enabled her to walk as she considered his faithfulness.

We don't worship to create an effect, but when we worship, faith grows in us. The Old Testament Hebrew word for meditate means to chew the cud. So when we meditate on Scripture, the truth of that Scripture gets hold of us. That's why it's often good to sing a song several times. This isn't mindless repetition, it's meditation and can inspire great faith in us.

God isn't primarily interested in worship. He's seeking worshippers — and that has to do with our relationship with him, expressing our love for him and knowing our security in him. We have the Holy Spirit and the word to enable us to bring him the kind of worship that he's looking for. Let's do that.

an ANOINTED PEOPLE

uestion: Why did God make you? Answer: For a personal and intimate relationship with himself. That's what makes you different from all other forms of creation. It's not that God needs your company, because he's self-sufficient, but there's something in his heart that longs for fellowship with you. Your greatest fulfilment comes when you draw near to him. You may not realise it, but God made you with the ability to relate to him in three different dimensions: the prophetic, the priestly and the kingly.

When I talk about being prophetic, I'm not referring to the gift of prophecy or about prophesying. The essence of being a prophetic person is this: you can hear God speak and declare his word to others. A prophet proclaims what God says to him and his prophetic gift develops as he listens and passes on what he hears. Adam was made with this prophetic dimension — he could communicate with God.

He was also made with a priestly dimension, which means that he could minister to God. On one occasion God rebuked his people saying, 'You have not ... lavished on me the fat of your sacrifices' (Is 43:24). This strange expression is picture language which tells us that our ministry to God somehow blesses him. As we give ourselves to him, serve him and express our love to him, he catches the aroma of our sacrifice and is blessed by it.

Finally, there's the kingly dimension. God has given us the right to rule and govern on his behalf. Adam was given authority over all the creatures and he started out by giving them all names.

So right at the beginning, God had a three dimensional relationship with man. The tragedy was that man sinned and deprived himself of all three dimensions. He lost the ability to hear God and his 'thinking became futile' (Rom 1:21). He couldn't minister to God because his sins made God hide his face 'so that he will not hear' (Is 59:2). And instead of ruling over creation, creation ruled over him. He had to control it 'by the sweat of [his] brow' (Gen 3:19).

OLD TESTAMENT RECOVERY

The Old Testament is a progressive recovery process. God spoke to various individuals who responded to him. But the climax came with Abraham. God made a covenant with him and restored all three dimensions. Abraham was a prophetic person. God told him, 'I will make you into a great nation and I will bless you; I will make your name great, and you will be a blessing' (Gen 12:2). He had a priestly function in that he built altars and ministered to God. 'The LORD appeared to Abram and said, "To your offspring I will give this land." So he built an altar there to the LORD, who had appeared to him' (Gen 12:7). He also had a kingly role because he led a large company of people. 'Abram acquired ... menservants and maidservants' (Gen 12:16).

God didn't just want one man to be a prophetic, priestly and kingly person, he wanted a nation of prophets, priests and kings. After the Exodus from Egypt, he promised the people through Moses, 'you will be for me a kingdom of priests' (Ex 19:6). What he was doing was giving the Israelites a vision of what it was like to be a New Covenant people who could hear him, speak to him and govern the nations for him.

Although God wanted all his people to minister to him, they couldn't do so because of sin. When Moses led them out of the camp to meet with God, they were so terrified of the manifestations of God's presence that they said to Moses, 'Speak to us yourself and we will listen. But do not have God speak to us or we will die' (Ex 20:19). So instead of enjoying an individual relationship with God, they relied on Aaron and the other priests to minister to God on their behalf. These priests wore special clothes which symbolised righteousness and holiness. They went through ceremonial washing which spoke of cleansing from sin and they were anointed with oil which separated them for their priestly functions. Certainly, God did speak to individuals like Gideon, Deborah, Samson and the prophets, but on the whole the ordinary people lived their spiritual lives through others whom God had anointed.

God also raised up prophets to hear his word and pass it on to the people. They often worked with the priests, but when the nation went through a time of backsliding, the prophets didn't prophesy and the priests didn't minister properly. The prophets were there to set the direction for the nation. and give them a moral code of conduct.

Then there were the kings. Originally it was God's plan to be the only leader of his people. But the Israelites clamoured for an earthly king, so God gave them Saul who started well but lost the kingdom through disobedience. The kings were meant to govern the nation on behalf of God. Some, like Hezekiah, Asa and Jehoshaphat, ruled fairly well. Others, like Ahab, Manasseh and Zedekiah, did not.

The greatest Old Testament king was David, 'a man after [God's] own heart' (1 Sam 13:14). God's heart was to have a people who would relate to him as prophets, priests and kings. David embodied all three of these. He was a prophetic man. Many of his psalms make prophetic statements about the kingdom of God and the Messiah's rule over the nations. 'I have installed my King on Zion, my holy hill ... Ask of me, and I will make the nations your inheritance, the ends of the earth your possession' (Ps 2:6,8). He also ministered to God as a priest. On one occasion he wore priestly robes and danced around in them. 'David, wearing a linen ephod, danced before the LORD with all his might' (2 Sam 6:14). And he was obviously 'king over Israel' (2 Sam 5:3).

The prophetic, priestly and kingly dimensions in David are reflected in the psalms. The prophetic element declares the greatness of God's character and his purposes in establishing the kingdom. David speaks prophetically when he speaks about the kingdom reaching the ends of the earth: 'All the nations you have made will come and worship before you. O Lord; they will bring glory to your name' (Ps 86:9).

David's psalms focus not so much on priestly animal sacrifices as on spiritual offerings of praise and joy: 'At his tabernacle will I sacrifice with shouts of joy; I will sing and make music to the LORD' (Ps 27:6). 'I will sacrifice a freewill offering to you' (Ps 54:6). 'May my prayer be set before you like incense; may the lifting up of my hands be like the evening sacrifice' (Ps 141:2).

The psalms also highlight the rule of God's people over the nations and the establishment of the kingdom of God:

May the praise of God be in their mouths and a double-edged sword in their hands, to inflict vengeance on the nations and punishment on the peoples, to bind their kings with fetters, their nobles with shackles of iron, to carry out the sentence written against them. This is the glory of all his saints' (Ps 149:6–9).

Of course, David wasn't perfect, but as he exercised his prophetic, priestly and kingly ministries, he pointed people to the one who embodied them perfectly — the Lord Jesus Christ. Psalm 110 speaks prophetically of the coming of Jesus and tells us that he is the greatest prophet, priest and king.

'The LORD says to my Lord:
"Sit at my right hand
until I make your enemies
a footstool for your feet."

The LORD will extend your mighty sceptre from Zion;
you will rule in the midst of your enemies.
Your troops will be willing on your day of battle.
Arrayed in holy majesty,
from the womb of the dawn
you will receive the dew of your youth.

The LORD has sworn and will not change his mind:
"You are a priest for ever,
in the order of Melchizedek."

The LORD is at your right hand;
he will crush kings on the day of his wrath.
He will judge nations, heaping up the dead
and crushing the rulers of the whole earth.
He will drink from a brook beside the way;
therefore he will lift up his head.'

THE ANOINTED MINISTRY OF JESUS

Adam lost the ability to relate to God as a prophet, priest and king. Jesus, the second Adam, restored all three ministries to us. The words, 'Messiah' and 'Christ' actually mean, 'the anointed one'. So when we read about Jesus being the Christ, we're actually saying, 'Here's the one whom God has anointed to be prophet, priest and king'. That's why Jesus began his earthly ministry by going into the synagogue in Nazareth and reading, 'The Spirit of the Lord is on me, because he has anointed me' (Lk 4:18). From this time on, he went out in his prophetic, priestly and kingly anointing.

When Jesus began his public ministry, he didn't just hear God's voice, he was himself the Word made flesh, the supreme prophet, God's voice to the human race. Jesus did nothing on his own initiative. He knew God's mind and told his disciples, 'I did not speak of my own accord, but the Father who sent me commanded me what to say and how to say it. I know that his command leads to eternal life. So whatever I say is just what the Father has told me to say' (Jn 12:49–50). Jesus awakened people out of their complacency, convicted them of sin and confirmed his message with signs, wonders and miracles. The people heard what he said, saw what he did and came to the conclusion, 'A great prophet has appeared among us' (Lk 7:16).

Jesus also came as a priest — to represent man to God. He was moved with compassion for his people and wept and interceded for them. 'O Jerusalem, Jerusalem, you who kill the prophets and stone those sent to you, how often I have longed to gather your children together, as a hen gathers her chicks under her wings, but you were not willing!' (Lk 13:34) He prayed for Peter, 'Simon, Simon, Satan has asked to sift you as wheat. But I have prayed for you' (Lk 22:31–32). He interceded for his disciples and for us, too 'I pray for them ...

I pray also for those who will believe in me through their message' (Jn 17:9,20).

But Jesus was more than a priest, he was also a victim. The high priest continually offered animal sacrifices for the sins of the people, but Jesus gave himself for us. 'Such a high priest meets our need — one who is holy, blameless, pure, set apart from sinners, exalted above the heavens. Unlike other high priests, he does not need to offer sacrifices day after day, first for his own sins, and then for the sins of the people. He sacrificed for their sins once for all when he offered himself' (Heb 7:26–27).

Then Jesus was anointed as a king. Wherever he went he preached about the kingdom of God. His message was the gospel of submission to a king and he exercised his kingly rule by confronting and defeating the powers of darkness. He said, 'If I drive out demons by the finger of God, then the kingdom of God has come to you' (Lk 11:20).

Jesus has always ruled. He's always been king. It's just that when he came to earth, he limited himself and functioned under the anointing of the Spirit. As a king he went to the cross and overcame all the demonic forces. He took the government away from Satan in the battle of Calvary. I was once casting out a demon. When I mentioned the cross, the demon started saying, 'Jesus is dead. We've got him. He's dead. We've killed him.' When I informed the demon that Jesus was risen, it fled.

After Jesus had risen and ascended, he was exalted at the right hand of the Father. From this time he began a new kind of rule as head over the church. God poured coronation oil on the head of his Son. It spilled down on his people on the Day of Pentecost and pours over us when we're baptised in the Holy Spirit.

An anointed people

Peter said, 'You are a chosen people, a royal priesthood, a holy nation, a people belonging to God' (1 Pet 2:9). He was referring back to the promise that God made to Moses, namely, 'you will be for me a kingdom of priests'. God's plan for us is far greater than our restoration as individuals. He's given us back what Adam lost by anointing us by his Spirit to be a company of people who function as prophets, priests and kings.

We're prophetic people. Our minds, which were once darkened by sin, have been changed. God has given us revelation and we can now think what he thinks and say what he says. That's why we need to read the Scriptures and Christian books. We train our minds to come into line with the mind of God, because we want to communicate his will to others. When we saturate ourselves in the truth about God, we'll find that what we declare is prophetic: our worship, evangelism, fellowship, preaching, the exercise of spiritual gifts and practical acts of service. All these things will speak truth about God.

We're priestly people. If we've been cleansed by the blood of Jesus, we can approach God and minister to him. We won't allow our emotions, anxieties or circumstances to hinder our worship. Rather, we'll lay these things aside and offer our sacrifice of praise simply because God has called us to worship him. We will also pray to God on behalf of others.

We're kingly people. God has called us to reign in life. We have victory over sin, temptation and demons, so the devil need never have the upper hand. He's been defeated and we're more than conquerors through Christ. When we proclaim release to the captives, heal the sick and cast out demons, we challenge Satan's rule and bring in God's kingdom.

If you know that you're a prophetic person, a priestly person and a kingly person, it will help you to be a better worshipper. What do I mean by that? Well, Peter goes on to say, 'that you may declare the praises of him who called you out of darkness into his wonderful light' (1 Pet 2:9). Worship is all bound up with understanding your prophetic, priestly and kingly function. The greater your understanding of who you are in Christ, the more you will want to worship and the greater will be your expectation in worship.

Let me encourage you. God has spoken to you and wants you to speak and live for him. He's taken away your sin and wants you to offer him your sacrifices of praise. He's given you power over the evil one and wants you to establish his kingdom wherever you are. So listen to God, minister to him and take authority in his name. That's your calling in Christ. That's what will put new zest into your worship. That's what will give you a more satisfying relationship with God than you've ever had before.

Chapter 6

Worship *and* Warfare

t was late. The minibus sped through the outskirts of London and along the M4. A few hours earlier, its occupants had been rehearsing for a Christian musical. Now they were on their way back to Basingstoke — a happy group of young people who were singing and laughing together.

Just as the minibus turned onto the Reading road, a car forced it into a lay-by and a menacing gang approached. One of them stood on the running board and declared evil intentions to those inside. The young people responded by worshipping the Lord in tongues. The effect wasn't immediate, but the gang left and the minibus arrived home safely.

God's presence was released into that potentially dangerous situation through the praises of the young people and also through the prayers of two of the wives in Basingstoke who had suddenly felt that the minibus was in danger. Praise is a weapon against the enemy. Satan is dethroned wherever God is enthroned.

Spiritual warfare is a controversial subject and people hold strong views about it. I haven't just read a considerable amount on the demonic, I've had a lot of experience in dealing with it — so I'm not just sharing theory, but principles that work. The fact is that when the presence of God comes, evil spirits always react. It's inevitable. One of the sad things is that we often don't experience enough of God's power in our worship to disturb the demons, so they stick around. Then, when God manifests himself in a new way, we see some demonic manifestations and people back off in fear.

I remember one Sunday morning when the power of God hit my local church in an extraordinary way. All over the building there were demonic manifestations and I ended up casting out demons until about 7.30 that evening. It was one of the most powerful meetings that I've ever been in, but for many it was initially a very frightening experience because they'd never seen anything like it before.

I've often felt like withdrawing from confrontation with demons. It's emotionally and spiritually draining and it can raise a lot of questions and create misunderstanding. But, as Jesus clearly shows, demons are real and will manifest themselves when he gets close to them. At some time we're bound to encounter them during worship, so it's better to be forewarned of this now than taken unawares when it happens. That's why I make no apology for mentioning spiritual warfare. It's a vital subject which we need to recover in church life and I want to help you understand it a bit better.

PRINCIPALITIES AND POWERS

Some people become preoccupied with warfare in the heavenlies and think, 'We must engage in this warfare through worship.' Is that right? Surely we don't worship God to create an effect. We worship him because of who he is and what he's done. We must be careful where we're focusing. When we worship God, principalities and powers will certainly be affected, but we must leave their fate to God. I believe that we engage the enemy in warfare by proclaiming the gospel.

There were very strong powers at work in Ephesus but Paul didn't bind the spirits of the goddess Diana. He preached the truth about Jesus, the demons came to light, he dealt with them and the people burnt their scrolls. The result was that the church grew to an estimated 60,000 people. Paul knew about the great cosmic conflict that was going on in Ephesus, that's why he later exhorted the Ephesians, 'Be strong in the Lord and in his mighty power. Put on the full armour of God so that you can take your stand against the devil's schemes' (Eph 6:10).

The first line of attack against Satanic powers is always through evangelism. You tell people that they need Jesus Christ. There's nothing wrong with going out on the streets, worshipping God and enjoying him together, but our praise marches will accomplish far more if we confront people with the gospel. It isn't a case of, 'God wins some battles, the devil wins others, but God will triumph in the end'. Jesus has already won the victory over the devil at the cross. John says, 'The reason the Son of God appeared was to destroy the devil's work' (1 Jn 3:8). Three historical acts and one future act all testify to the defeat of Satan:

1. Calvary.
2. The resurrection when Jesus demonstrated his power over death.
3. The ascension when Jesus went into heaven and is now seated at the right hand of God. His enemies have been made his footstool and he must rule until they're all under his feet.
4. The consummation of the ages when Jesus comes again.

Jesus tells us, 'No-one can enter a strong man's house unless he first ties up the strong man. Then he can rob his house' (Mk 3:27). The verb translated, 'tie up' is used in only one other place in the New Testament where it refers to Satan's being bound for a thousand years (Rev 20:2). There are differing millenial views about the interpretation of this passage of scripture. However, many theologians believe that this thousand years refers to the present church age. In other words, Jesus bound Satan at Calvary and Satan will remain bound until Jesus returns. When we declare that the devil is bound, we're not saying that he can't do anything. Rather, we're saying that he's restricted to a certain sphere of activity. God is totally in control but he still allows Satan to have a limited amount of authority. The enemy has three lines of attack: the world, the flesh and the devil.

First, he encourages us to adopt the world's values. Some people think that it's worldly to go to the cinema or to a football match on Sundays, or for girls to wear make-up. But worldliness is an attitude. It's about thinking and making decisions by society's value system. Second, the enemy encourages us to use our bodies to engage in sin — sexual sin and over indulgence in food and drink. Finally, he comes to us in a more direct way. When we experience a time of unexplained depression, fear, or sickness, we're actually going through a 'day of evil' (Eph 6:13) when Satan is trying to pull us down.

Few of us are actually troubled by Satan himself because he's a created being and, unlike God, can only be in one place at a time. I can recall just one occasion when I may have had a personal encounter with the Evil One. Rosie and I had a girl living with us who was severely anorexic and alcoholic. Her bedroom was above ours and one night she tried to take her life. I was in bed when I suddenly felt as though I was going to choke to death. I called on the name of Jesus and the enemy departed, but it would have been a very frightening experience had I not had the presence of mind to use my God-given authority.

There's a hierarchy in the spirit realm. Some principalities are good and others are evil. Paul says that God's intent was 'that now, through the church, the manifold wisdom of God should be made known to the rulers and authorities in the heavenly realms' (Eph 3:10). The rulers and authorities here could be good as well as evil. But elsewhere the powers to which Paul refers are definitely evil — which is the case when he says, 'our struggle is not against flesh and blood, but against the rulers, against the authorities, against the powers of this dark world and against the spiritual forces of evil in the heavenly realms' (Eph 6:12). These principalities and powers are graded in terms of how evil they are, and they rule over things like politics, communism, racism and capitalism.

There are principalities that can sometimes govern geographical areas. This subject is rather controversial, but it's referred to in the Bible. When Daniel was praying, an angel tried to respond to him but was detained by the prince of Persia (Dan 10:13). When Jesus was on earth, demonic activity was quite common in the region of Caesarea Philippi because it was known for its occult worship. The Gadarene demoniac lived in this area and it's possible that a demonic force stirred up the water when the disciples were trying to row across the lake (Mk 4:39).

There can be principalities and powers behind families. If there's a history of illness, poverty or unexplained accidents, this can be due to a curse over a family. A friend and I once prayed for an Indian man with severe curvature of the spine who expected to be confined to a wheelchair for his whole life. We discerned that there was a demonic curse over his family and my friend actually got the name of the power behind it. We bound the evil power and the man was healed immediately.

Our struggle isn't against flesh and blood, so we need to start looking beyond what man is doing. Behind the world's system there are principalities and powers which are trying to manipulate what's going on, and sometimes we'll be the target for their attack. We must understand these things if we're going to build strong churches, see revival and move in the power and authority of God. We must also remember that God has total authority over the enemy which is secured through the death, resurrection, ascension and eventual return of his Son.

Spiritual warfare is closely linked with worship. We've been called to bring in the kingdom of God, so we will naturally have to cast out evil spirits. The disciples in the New Testament did this, but it's a principle in the whole of Scripture. Many of the psalms speak about exalting the name of God and bringing victory over the enemy (Ps 68).

The problem with this is that some people think, 'All you have to do is praise the Lord whatever happens. Then the enemy is driven away and the problems disappear.' Theologically this is far too superficial. If we're going to be kingdom people and implement the victory of God over Satan, we need to learn some spiritual principles and discover how to use our weapons effectively.

THE THREAT OF A STRONG ENEMY

Many worship leaders use 2 Chronicles 20:1–30 to illustrate how praise drives out the enemy. Actually, there's much more to the story than that. The passage contains some very important truths which will help us to understand both our victory over Satan and the place of praise in our conflict with him. First, let's look at the history behind 2 Chronicles 20.

Just before God took the Israelites into the Promised Land, he made a covenant with them. He said that if they obeyed him, he would bless them by giving them peace, prosperity and rest from their enemies. But he added that if they disobeyed him, he would curse them. When God curses someone, he takes his hand off a situation and allows the enemy to control it.

The nation sinned against God and was split into two — Israel and Judah. 'Judah', which means 'praise', was the more righteous and much smaller kingdom. At this point in time, its ruler was Jehoshaphat who was essentially a good king, except that he'd made one vital mistake: he'd disobeyed God by marrying into the house of Ahab. Because of this unholy alliance 'the wrath of the LORD' was upon him (2 Chron 19:2). So when the Moabites and Ammonites made war on Judah, the people were frightened. They shouldn't have been in this state because they had the covenant promises of God. But because of Jehoshaphat's sin, they were under a curse and God allowed the enemy to come against them.

This may help us to answer the question, 'Can Christians be demonised?' When Jesus came to earth, he should have encountered a covenant people who were living under God's blessing. But for about four hundred years they'd been disobedient and were now living under his curse. When a crippled woman came to Jesus he released her from a Satanic spirit and called her a 'daughter of Abraham' (Lk 13:16). This was a covenant name, so in New Testament terms, he was referring to her as one of God's people.

The scriptural principle is this: if we break a covenant, we open ourselves up to a curse. In a New Testament sense, if we deliberately sin, we court the demonic — which is why a fair amount of counselling involves deliverance. Christians aren't possessed by demons — the Greek word, *daimonitzomai*, means to have a demon, not to be possessed by one. However, sometimes Christians can be troubled by the demonic.

In this Old Testament story, the Ammonites and Moabites represent the work of Satan and his principalities and powers who were threatening God's authority and the people's inheritance. This speaks of what's happening in the church today. We're on the edge of some very serious confrontation — particularly on the issues of abortion and homosexuality. If we stand against these things, we're in for a tough time because we're cutting right across what people think today. We need to know how we can come against the enemy.

Spiritual warfare begins the moment we're converted. Things that didn't trouble us before suddenly become temptations and we find that we're having to battle our way through. This is quite normal. We're wrestling against principalities and powers, which is why we must put on the whole armour of God. Some people say, 'You put on the armour piece by piece every day.' I'd like to suggest that we live in it — because we're in Christ. Every day we make sure that we remember who we are, that we've got our doctrine right, that we're obeying the Scriptures, witnessing, praying and worshipping God. That's really what it's all about.

THE ENEMY'S IDENTITY

I don't want to dwell too much on Satan, but it's helpful to know a bit about him so that we can understand how he operates. At one time, he was a beautiful created being who led the worship in heaven. We read, 'the workmanship of thy tabrets and of thy pipes was prepared in thee in the day that thou wast created' (Ezek 28:13 RSV). But he wasn't satisfied with worshipping God, he wanted to be like God. When his heart became proud, God threw him out of heaven (see Is 14:12–21; Ezek 28:1–19).

The Bible gives Satan several names. It's probably easiest just to list them.

> *Accuser* (Rev 12:10)
> *Tempter* (Mt 4:3; 1 Thess 3:5)
> *Dragon and Serpent* (Rev 12:9)
> *Destroyer* (Rev 9:11)
> *Ruler of the kingdom of the air* (Eph 2:2)
> *Beelzebub — Lord of the flies* (Mt 10:25)
> *Prince of this world* (Jn 12:31; 14:30; 16:11)
> *The evil one* (Mt 6:13; 13:19)

He also has several characteristics. Again, I'll just mention these.

He's bound (Mk 3:27)

He's strong
He assails people's spirits with lust, pride and hatred (Lk 4:5–7)
He assails their bodies with disease, torture and death (Job 2:7; 13:16; Heb 2:14)
He assails the institutions of men with structural evil, e.g. politics and education (2 Cor 10:5–6)
He manipulates nations (Dan 10:12–13,20)
He manipulates city councils (1 Thess 2:18)
He manipulates rioting mobs (Jn 8:44–59)
He manipulates the elements (Mk 4:39)

He's violent (Lk 9:39)

He's highly intelligent and subtle (2 Cor 2:11; 2 Tim 2:26)

He's a liar (Jn 8:44)

He dominates (1 Jn 5:19)

He's persistent (Lk 4:1–13)

We can see many of these characteristics in the Moabite/Ammonite army that was threatening Judah (2 Chron 20).

GOD'S STRATEGY FOR VICTORY

God had a way of dealing with Judah's enemies. We can learn from this as we come against spiritual powers.

1. ANOINTED LEADERSHIP

King

Jehoshaphat was a spiritual king who knew that he had to pray. When some people pray in prayer meetings, they can be over familiar with God and almost dictate to him what he should do. Certainly, we should remind God from his word what he's said and pray these scriptures into situations, but we must never tell him what to do to bring glory to his name. Jehoshaphat prayed, 'O LORD, God of our fathers, are you not the God who is in heaven? You rule over all the kingdoms of the nations' (2 Chron 20:6).

His prayer was very bold, but it honoured God. The king had a tremendous understanding of who God was and feared him.

After Jehoshaphat had addressed God, he began reasoning with him, saying effectively, 'Lord, you brought us out of

Egypt. Surely, you didn't do that so we could be destroyed by the enemy. We were kind to these people, but now they're coming against us and it's not right.' This was kingdom praying. It focused on the majesty of God and on his purpose, but it never lost the sense of awe and respect.

Prophet

Once the king had prayed, the prophet began to prophesy. We read, 'Then the Spirit of the LORD came upon Jahaziel son of Zechariah' (2 Chron 20:14). Jahaziel was a man of insight — God spoke to him. But he also faced reality — there was a real army that needed defeating. First, he encouraged the people, 'Listen, King Jehoshaphat and all who live in Judah and Jerusalem! This is what the LORD says to you: "Do not be afraid or discouraged because of this vast army"' (v. 15). Then he reminded them of the truth, 'For the battle is not yours, but God's'. He outlined God's strategy, 'Take up your positions; stand firm and see the deliverance the LORD will give you' (v. 17). And finally, he encouraged them again, 'Do not be afraid; do not be discouraged.'

Priests

When the king was ruling properly and the prophets were speaking out God's word, the priests began to minister to the Lord. They 'stood up and praised the LORD, the God of Israel, with a very loud voice' (2 Chron 20:19). God was restoring the ministries of prophet, priest and king. The principle is clear: if we want to overcome the enemy, our spiritual leaders need to get their act together.

2. ANOINTED PEOPLE

There wasn't only strong leadership, there was also an obedient people. Everyone — women and children included

— stood before the Lord, worshipped him and obeyed what he said. As we've already said, God wants us to be prophets, priests and kings. So if we're going to be victorious, we must as individuals, listen to him, minister to him and take authority in his name. What's true of us as individuals should be true of us corporately too. The people of Judah came together to hear God, worship him and defeat the enemy in his name.

So God's strategy for victory wasn't simply: 'Get your instruments, go out and praise me.' It involved far more than that. God wasn't giving his people a technique to overcome the enemy. He was building a people. In New Testament terms, he was restoring the church.

THE COMPLETENESS OF OUR VICTORY

As the people responded to God, the enemy began to fight itself. Evidently, something went on in the heavenlies that had nothing to do with the people. They just obeyed the Lord and worshipped him. He stepped in to give the victory and all they had to do was carry off the plunder.

The people sang, 'Give thanks to the LORD, for his love endures for ever' (2 Chron 20:21). They focused on the character of God, not on binding principalities and powers in the heavenlies. Similarly, our primary emphasis should be to address God rather than the enemy. Acknowledging his greatness and exalting him is often sufficient to overcome principalities and powers because they hate worship. When Peter says, '... that you may declare the praises of him who called you ...' (1 Pet 2:9) the Greek word translated 'declare' has a military flavour. It means, 'declare so that the enemy hears and trembles'. So when we praise the Lord, something happens in the heavenlies. We leave that battle with God and get on with reaching out to people who don't know him.

Sometimes the enemy erects strongholds. These can be personal things, world systems or ideologies and we need to know how to pull them down. This is a sensitive subject and we must be careful how we handle it because there's a lot of unreality associated with so-called 'spiritual warfare'.

Some Christians label Brighton as a place where people come for a dirty weekend and say that there's a stronghold of pleasure and sex over it. If this is true, it needs to be broken, but I don't think we'll break it by binding a principality over the town. The stronghold will crumble as we declare the gospel and live by it. We must remember that it's through the church that the manifold wisdom of God is made known to the principalities and powers.

It's far more likely that God himself will pull down strongholds where the leadership is right and where the people obey him and glorify him for who he is. Jesus said, 'I will build my church, and the gates of Hades will not overcome it' (Mt 16:18). We gain the victory over the enemy in many different ways. It's just as aggressive to refuse to give in to lying, cheating and stealing as it is to march around with banners singing and shouting God's praises. It's just as aggressive to sing 'Jesus, how lovely you are' as it is it to sing 'Terrible as an army with banners.' God wants us consistently to make inroads into enemy territory and establish his kingdom on earth.

When we proclaim the kingdom, we must remember that external circumstances won't always change. Some Christians were fed to the lions. They sang songs of praise to God and heard the roar of the crowds against them. But the principalities and powers behind those crowds weren't stopped and the believers triumphed not through life but through death. Thankfully, it's not always like that. Praise will win some wonderful victories. I've been in many situations where people have been worshipping and God has moved with great power.

One of the great things about David is that he was both a warrior and a poet, an aggressive man and a tender man. Jesus is like that. Let me encourage you to have a fighting spirit and a gentle spirit — particularly in the area of praise and worship. When God is enthroned on your praises, Satan's rule will be thwarted. So live by the word, declare truth in your worship, and expect God to come against the principalities and powers which undoubtedly exist in your area and nation.

the OLD *in the* NEW?

People often say to me, 'How can you use Old Testament worship to justify what we do in our worship times today? You focus a lot on what the Israelites did in the time of David, but where do you find things like shouting, clapping, dancing and using musical instruments in the New Testament? Is it right to take worship under the Old Covenant and apply it to the New?' It's an important issue and I want to address it. But before I do that I'd like to get to the heart of worship because once you understand that, you'll be able to see more clearly how God wants us to worship him today.

GOD'S DWELLING PLACE

God wants to live among his people. This theme runs right the way through the Bible. In Genesis we see Adam relating with God in the Garden of Eden. We read that 'Enoch walked with God' (Gen 5:24) and that 'Noah found favour in the eyes of the LORD' (Gen 6:8). When Jacob had a revelation of God, he said, 'Surely the LORD is in this place ... How awesome is this place!' (Gen 28:16,17) So strong was the sense of God's presence that Jacob called the place Bethel — house of God.

God wanted to live among his people during their forty years' wanderings in the wilderness, so he commanded Moses to erect a Tabernacle — literally, 'dwelling place' where he could manifest his presence. This Tabernacle was actually a tent within a tent. The inner section was called the Holy of holies and it contained the ark of the covenant. This ark was a large intricately designed box which housed the two tablets of stone on which were inscribed the Ten Commandments, a jar of manna — the food which God supplied to sustain the people in the wilderness, and Aaron's rod which budded supernaturally. These things actually represent New Testament ideas. The Ten Commandments speak of the law, the manna speaks of feeding on Christ and the rod speaks of resurrection life.

When the Israelites first left Egypt, the tribes were arranged in such a way that they formed a giant cross with the ark of the covenant at the head. We read that:

> 'Whenever the ark set out, Moses said, "Rise up, O LORD! Let your enemies be scattered, And let those who hate you flee before you"' (Num 10:35 NKJV).

Only on one day in the year — the day of atonement — could the high priest go into the Holy of holies where God's manifest presence, or shekinah glory, hovered. On that occasion, the priest had to put on special clothes and carry out an elaborate sacrificial ritual before he could enter God's presence and pray for the people. Hebrew history tells us that the Jews were so frightened of entering God's presence that they used to tie a piece of rope around the priest's leg in case he died in the Holy of holies and they had to get him out! So the Tabernacle became the focal point for the nation's spiritual life. When the psalmist says, 'Enter his gates with thanksgiving and his courts with praise,' he's calling people to come into the gates and courts of the Tabernacle.

When the Israelites entered the promised land they set up the Tabernacle at Shiloh, where Eli ministered and where God called Samuel. After a time of backsliding, the Israelites were defeated by the Philistines who captured the ark, the symbol of God's presence among his people, and put it in their temple to Dagon. Since God's presence was still with the ark, the statue of Dagon fell over in front of it and the people were afflicted with tumours. When the Philistines realised that God's hand was against them, they sent the ark back to Israel where it remained at the home of Abinadab for twenty years.

When David became king of Israel, there was one place in the Promised Land that had not been conquered — Mount Zion — which was in the hands of the Jebusites. David attacked the Jebusites and drove them out. Then he established Mount Zion, or the City of David, as the capital of the nation. We know this place as Jerusalem. David planned to bring the ark of the covenant back to Jerusalem and establish a place of worship there.

His first attempt at bringing back the ark failed. According to the Mosaic law, the ark should have been carried, but it was placed on a cart. When the oxen stumbled, a man called Uzzah steadied the ark with his hand and was struck dead. Three months later David brought the ark to Jerusalem in the prescribed way and danced with all his might.

'All Israel brought up the ark of the covenant of the LORD with shouts, with the sounding of rams' horns and trumpets, and of cymbals, and the playing of lyres and harps' (1 Chron 15:28).

Most Bible historians suggest that David wrote Psalm 68 on this occasion. The Psalm begins:

> *'Let God arise, Let his enemies be scattered; Let those also who hate him flee before him' (Ps 68:1 NKJV).*

Clearly, David was remembering how Moses and the Israelites used to set out with the ark, and was then applying it to the entry of the ark into Jerusalem.

Both events point forward to the onward purpose of God, the establishment of his kingdom and the rule of Christ over the nations. Jesus said that one of the signs of the last days would be this: the 'gospel of the kingdom will be preached in the whole world as a testimony to all nations, and then the end will come' (Mt 24:14). The Greek word translated, 'nations' means every ethnic group. There are many ethnic groups which haven't yet heard the gospel. But we believe that in the end times, God will pour out his Spirit and bring into his kingdom a people from 'every nation, tribe, people and language' (Rev 7:9).

When David prophesied these things, he was speaking far beyond his people's understanding. They were under the impression that God's purposes were bound up in Israel and regarded all the other nations as their enemies. David, however, envisaged something far greater and declared, 'Sing to God, O kingdoms of the earth' (Ps 68:32). The whole psalm speaks of the prophetic purposes of God.

So when David saw the ark rising up, he also saw God arising and moving on. In the rest of the psalm he prophesied about the coming of Jesus to establish his kingdom on Mount Zion and spoke about the church age. He even prophesied about church leadership, saying:

> *'When you ascended on high, you led captives in your train; you received gifts from men, even from the rebellious — that you, O LORD God, might dwell there'* (Ps 68:18).

David was actually speaking about his victory over the Jebusites, but his words also find fulfilment in Jesus' exaltation and the triumph of the gospel through the church. Paul quotes verse 18 when he speaks of the risen Christ establishing church government through the ministries of apostle, prophet, evangelist and pastor/teacher (Eph 4:11).

From the time when David brought the ark into Jerusalem, he had a new revelation about the place of praise and worship in the nation. His Tabernacle became the centre of creativity, music, singing, dancing and rejoicing.

David wanted to build a house for God, but that task fell to his son Solomon. Once Solomon's Temple was built, Davidic worship was transferred there. The nation experienced several times of backsliding, but whenever they returned to God there was a restoration of worship. A king and his people would return to the Law of Moses, 'with rejoicing and singing, as David had ordered' (2 Chron 23:18).

When Solomon's Temple was knocked down, another was built to replace it, but this second Temple was never restored to its former glory. There was no sense of the supernatural presence of God in it, nor was there any sign of the shekinah glory which had hovered over the ark of the covenant in the Holy of holies. The high priest was unable to communicate with God and for 400 years the nation went through a time of spiritual poverty. The second Temple was followed by Herod's Temple which was barely finished when it was destroyed by the Romans in 70AD.

The prophets often challenged the sinfulness of their day and warned of impending judgement, but they also foretold a time of restoration which went far beyond what happened historically. They pointed to a new age when the gentile nations would worship God, when the focus would no longer be on a vulnerable physical building, but on a permanent spiritual temple — the church. Paul says:

> *'In him the whole building is joined together and rises to become a holy temple in the Lord. And in him you too are being built together to become a dwelling in which God lives by his Spirit'* (Eph 2:21–22).

The Greek word which he uses for 'temple' is the same word that is used for 'Holy of holies' in the Greek version of the Old Testament. God manifested his presence in the Holy of holies. As individuals, we're temples of the Holy Spirit. As local churches, we're being built together to manifest the presence of God who dwells within us. If God's glory came down and filled the Temple in the Old Testament, how much more will his glory fall when his people come together to worship him under the New Covenant?

So the dwelling place of God went through seven stages: Moses' Tabernacle, the Tabernacle at Shiloh, David's Tabernacle, Solomon's Temple, the second Temple, Herod's Temple and the church.

THE TABERNACLE OF DAVID

God wants to restore his church and fill it with his glory. To understand something of what that means, we really need to return to the Tabernacle of David and look at the freedom, simplicity and vitality that surrounded the Israelites' worship there.

There was one very significant difference between the Tabernacle of Moses and the Tabernacle of David. The Tabernacle of Moses was based on law and ritual. The high priest had to offer sacrifices on behalf of the people because they weren't allowed to go into the Holy of holies. Although there were still sacrifices at David's Tabernacle, the emphasis wasn't on sacrifice, but on worship, praise and prophesying with musical instruments. The ark of the covenant was in full view and anyone could enter. This new wave of spirituality didn't last long, but it remained long enough to give us a glimpse of New Covenant life — everyone freely enjoying the presence of God through a new and living way by the blood of Jesus.

There was an interesting kind of structure in Davidic worship. At the top, if you like, was David the king and musical prophet. Then there was Kenaniah, who was 'in charge of the singing' because 'he was skilful at it,' (1 Chron 15:22). Asaph, Heman and Jeduthun were 'set apart for the ministry of prophesying, accompanied by harps, lyres and cymbals' (1 Chron 25:1). They had twenty-four sons whom they trained in music, and these sons each trained twelve members of their own families. This made a group of 288 musicians who were skilful in singing, playing instruments and prophecy. In addition, there were 4,000 priests who worshipped the Lord day and night. So there was a great musical orchestra leading the worship, and a people who learned from them how to praise the Lord.

It was in this context that the psalms were written — not to be read, but to be sung. Maybe the psalms started out like this: David strolls out on the hills with his harp. He looks out over the valleys, sees the sheep and begins to play his harp and sing, 'The Lord is my shepherd'. When he arrives back at the Tabernacle, he calls out, 'Kenaniah, I've just written a great new worship song.' Then he sings it and the two of them add some more chords and teach it to Asaph, Heman and Jeduthun. As the five men sit there, the Spirit moves on them and they begin to sing prophecy to one another around the words of David. Then they teach the song to their families and it isn't long before 288 people know it and are teaching it to the rest of the congregation. Together the people follow the various instructions in the psalms — singing, raising their hands, bowing, kneeling, dancing, bursting into joyful applause, shouting, joining in a refrain, or lying prostrate before the Lord. These instructions are there for us too. They're meant to create variety as we come together to worship God.

WHAT'S THE ANSWER?

We have a problem with worship in the early church — very little is said about it, although there are some hints in 1 Corinthians 12 and 14, Ephesians 5:18 and Colossians 3:16. Post New Testament church history is silent apart from a few comments on how to break bread and take up the offering. So, to repeat the question at the beginning of this chapter, is it right to take worship under the Old Covenant and apply it to the New? I think that the answer lies in Acts 15:12–21.

At this time in the early church, there were certain people who were insisting that new converts had to be circumcised according to the Mosaic law. The leaders of the church in Jerusalem got together to discuss the issue and James summed up for them. It's important to remember that his comments related to grace rather than worship, but it's grace that releases us into worship. Under the inspiration of the Holy Spirit, James was using an Old Testament scripture about grace and linking it with worship. Quoting the prophecy of Amos, he said, 'I will return and rebuild David's fallen tent' (Acts 15:16) and applied it to the church.

Some people take this restoration of David's Tabernacle literally. They put on priestly robes, parade around with an ark, blow rams' horns and sing modern songs. But the application isn't literal, it's spiritual. We don't just take things out of the old and stick them into the new. Rather, we observe what's behind the form of Davidic worship and apply it in a setting of grace.

The early Christians lived under grace, but I can't believe that when they read a psalm about singing and shouting to the Lord they thought, 'Oh, that's an interesting idea from the Old Testament.' They'd respond to it by singing and shouting — because they were filled with the Holy Spirit and he inspires worship. On the Day of Pentecost, the crowd was first attracted by praise, not preaching. It was worship that led to evangelism (Acts 2:1–13).

While the Israelites were in captivity in Babylon, they obviously couldn't go to the Temple in Jerusalem, so they established small places of worship around Babylon. These places came to be known as synagogues. When the people returned to the promised land, they continued the practice of going to the synagogue every Sabbath and just went to the Temple once a year. In the synagogue they read the law, sang psalms and then praised God together. Jesus himself went to the synagogue to worship God.

The singing of psalms was clearly part of Jewish life. The word 'psalm' means 'to twitch over the strings' so it was always accompanied by instruments. So when Paul exhorted the Ephesians:

'Speak to one another with psalms, hymns and spiritual songs. Sing and make music in your heart to the Lord' (Eph 5:19), it's likely that the early Christians did just that. The Bible simply gives us a historical record of their worship. While it's true that we don't read about instruments in the New Testament, the idea is certainly there.

Worship at the Tabernacle of David is mirrored in the book of Revelation. There were twenty-four sons who led the worship in David's Tabernacle and twenty-four elders who lead the worship in heaven (Rev 5:8). It's significant that elders are mentioned here. It's an eldership responsibility to oversee the worshipping church. Of course, not every elder will be a worship leader, but they will all be responsible for praise and worship in the church. Surely, the ability to worship is a key qualification for spiritual leadership.

John says, 'I heard what sounded like a great multitude, like the roar of rushing waters' (Rev 19:6). It's been suggested that this revelation was based on what he'd heard when the church worshipped together — a combination of musical instruments, singing, shouting and exaltation. Apparently, the praise of the martyrs as they went into the arena in Rome was greater than the baying of the crowd for their blood. Worship was evidently central in the life of the early church.

There's no doubt about it, the Christians in the New Testament were a company of singing, praising, worshipping people. Their worship was based on the synagogue style, but was injected with the life and vitality of the Spirit. They sang psalms and hymns, and their spiritual songs would have been both composed and spontaneous. They'd have been songs based on the psalms, songs of personal testimony, and songs in tongues. Within this context of worship, the believers would have exercised spiritual gifts: words of wisdom and knowledge, acts of faith, healing, miracles, prophecy, discerning of spirits, tongues, interpretation of tongues and giving. They'd also have heard teaching on the Scriptures.

If Davidic worship under the Old Covenant was varied and exciting, it's hard to imagine that the worship in the early church was dull by comparison. The New Testament Christians were under grace and had been anointed by the Spirit, so the singing of the psalms couldn't possibly have been formal and lifeless! The psalms exhort God's people to:

> *Bless the Lord*
> *Praise the Lord*
> *Sing to the Lord*
> *Clap your hands*
> *Lift up your hands*
> *Bow down*
> *Worship*
> *Give thanks*
> *Magnify his name*
> *Shout to God*
> *Shout joyfully with psalms*
> *Dance*
> *Kneel*
> *Praise the Lord with instruments*

God has given us creative ways of worshipping him. We don't know what New Testament worship sounded like, but we can assume that the infant church was creative in its worship. Spirit-filled believers would have sung, clapped their hands, danced, shouted and knelt before God — and these things are meant for us to do too.

God said, 'I will return and rebuild David's fallen tent' (Acts 15:16). 'I will return' speaks of God's presence with his people. Just as the shekinah glory hovered over David's Tabernacle, so now God's dwelling place is with his church. He wants to 'rebuild David's fallen tent' — not in a literal way, but in a spiritual one. He wants to build us together so that we 'become a dwelling in which [he] lives by his Spirit' (Eph 2:22).

So yes, provided we handle it carefully, we can take worship under the Old Covenant and apply it to the New. Paul referred back to the Old Testament when he exhorted the Ephesians to speak to one another with psalms, hymns and spiritual songs. And John did the same when he looked back to Davidic worship and saw it mirrored in God's revelation to him.

I vividly remember one occasion when I took a worship situation from the Old Testament and translated it into the New. It was at one of the Downs Bible Weeks and Terry Virgo was preaching about Nehemiah and the rebuilding of the wall of Jerusalem. Nehemiah wanted to restore Davidic worship, so when the wall was finished he brought the Levites together to celebrate its dedication 'with songs of thanksgiving and with the music and cymbals, harps and lyres' (Neh 12:27). He also summoned the singers from their villages around Jerusalem. After the people had purified themselves, the leaders and two large choirs went up on the wall. One choir processed to the right, the other to the left. As they marched, they sang and played their musical instruments with such enthusiasm that 'the sound of rejoicing in Jerusalem could be heard far away' (Neh 12:43).

Before the Bible Week I began to seek God about how to lead the worship after Terry had preached on this passage and God gave me a revelation of instruments making a joyful noise, of singing and worship. What I wanted to do was recreate this great event by catching the spirit of the two choirs as they praised God, so I took some of the words from the song of Moses and set them in a round. After Terry had preached, I divided the congregation into two sorts of choirs, each singing a separate part, then I got the musicians to accompany them. There was a clear tune, but I gave the musicians some space for improvisation, so that we could have some crashing noises from the cymbals and fanfares from the brass instruments. From time to time I sang prophetically over the top of everything. It turned out to be a glorious worship time. God is a God of creativity, of vitality, of life and power. Let's see this reflected in our worship times.

CHAPTER 8

WHAT is WORSHIP?

There's a problem: English speakers are limited by their vocabulary. When the Old Testament speaks about people rejoicing before God, we translate this as 'praise' or 'worship'. We don't realise that in the original Hebrew there are lots of words for worship and that they all have different shades of meaning.

Tozer called worship 'the missing jewel of the church'. Each Hebrew word for worship is like one facet of that jewel and together they bring the sort of colour, sparkle and rich variety that we should see reflected in our personal and corporate times of worship. It may sound uninspiring to go through these words, but I assure you that it's not. If you know what they mean, see them in their context and meditate on them, you will have a broader understanding of what worship is all about — and that should make you a better worshipper.

True worship springs from deep within the heart and is expressed in our relationship with God and also with others. It should actually affect everything that we do — in church life and outside it. We worship God and work out that worship by loving one another. If we're critical or negative with others, we're not really expressing our worship to God. So a good definition of worship is: 'Loving God in the presence of His people and loving God's people in the presence of God.'

Shacah

All true worship is based on the Old Testament word, *shacah*, which means to bow down in reverence, to prostrate oneself. *Shacah* is often used to denote coming before God in worship. When the enslaved Israelites 'heard that the Lord was concerned about them and had seen their misery, they bowed down and worshipped' (Ex 4:31). Bowing is an attitude of submission and obedience, it involves giving ourselves unreservedly to God.

Hallel

To be boastful, to praise, to celebrate. *Hallel* is found more than 160 times in the Old Testament and Psalms 113–118 are referred to as the Hallel Psalms. They give particular praise to God for the deliverance of Israel from Egypt, which is why the Jews traditionally sang them on the eve of the Passover. After the Lord's Supper, Jesus and his disciples sang a hymn (Mt 26:30) which was probably one of these psalms. It's amazing to think that as Jesus went to the cross he was meditating on words like 'This is the day the LORD has made; let us rejoice and be glad in it' (Ps 118:24).

The word, *yah* is an abbreviated form of Yahweh, the Old Testament name for God. When *hallel* and *yah* are combined, they form the word, *hallelujah* which means 'praise the Lord'. Hallelujah can be used as an explosion of enthusiasm — in the same way as a football crowd erupts when someone scores a goal.

Yadah

To give thanks, to praise. The root of this word suggests the extended hand and therefore implies worshipping with raised hands. The word originated with the birth of one of Jacob's sons. We read, '[Rachel] conceived again, and when she gave birth to a son she said, "This time I will praise the LORD." So she named him Judah' (Gen. 29:35). The tribe of Judah was particularly used in praise. When the Israelites moved across the desert, Judah led the way — praise always comes first. David was from Judah (1 Sam 17:12), and Jesus was the Lion of the tribe of Judah (Rev 5:5).

A few years ago it was a radical thing to raise your hands in a Sunday meeting. Now we've got so used to it that we're in danger of becoming complacent about it. The Greek word for man is *anthropos*, which means 'upward looker'. Sinful man is naturally a downward looker. Cain's offering to God was tainted by sin (1 Jn 3:12) and when God rejected it, Cain's face was 'downcast' (Gen 4:5). When are sins are forgiven, we look up and the raising of our hands emphasises that we're coming to God without any sense of fear, guilt or condemnation.

Yadah also means to acknowledge in public or to praise the Lord publicly. David declared, 'I will give you thanks in the great assembly' among throngs of people I will praise you' (Ps 35:18). The word translated 'praise' here is *yadah*.

Todah

To give thanks. This word embraces the idea of thanksgiving and is often used in a setting where many people are singing songs of thanksgiving together. 'I remember ... leading the procession to the house of God, with shouts of joy and thanksgiving among the festive throng' (Ps 42:4). When the walls of Jerusalem were built, Nehemiah 'assigned two large choirs to give thanks' (Neh 12:31).

Tehillah

A song of praise particularly extolling deeds which are worthy of praise (*Tehillim* is the Hebrew title for the book of Psalms). It also refers to someone's attributes: 'He is your praise; he is your God, who performed for you those great and awesome wonders you saw with your own eyes' (Deut 10:21). *Tehillah* is about praising God for his actions and for who he is.

We need times of *tehillah* type praise in our worship. The best way to extol God's character is to meditate on his attributes — his faithfulness, compassion, justice, grace, etc. Let's learn scriptures about each attribute so that when we come to worship, we're singing songs from a knowledge of God.

At David's Tabernacle there was a man called Jeduthun who 'prophesied, using the harp in thanking and praising the LORD' (1 Chron 25:3). So there's a close link between prophesying and giving thanks to God. Let me encourage you to meditate on God's character and then to release songs of thanksgiving to God for who he is and what he's done. Do this in private first, then be open for God to use you in a more public setting. You needn't just sing about 'religious' themes like deliverance from the Red Sea. Thank God for healing you or for giving you things. Use everyday words to express your feelings and enjoy yourself.

Tehillah also means to praise publicly by singing. David says, 'I will declare your name to my brothers; in the congregation I will praise you' (Ps 22:22). Jesus quotes this verse in Hebrews 2:12 and sings a song of thanksgiving to the Father about us. That's a mind-blowing idea.

Tehillah is also a technical musical term for a song of praise. Psalm 145 is a *tehillah*. It extols God's character and his deeds. Why not note down all the attributes of God in this Psalm and meditate on them?

Barak

To bless. This usually speaks of God's covenant in pouring out His blessing on mankind. It's also an expression of praise: 'Blessed be God Most High, who delivered your enemies into your hand' (Gen 14:20). 'Bless the LORD, O my soul; and all that is within me, bless his holy name!' (Ps 103:1 RSV) There's great power behind blessing and cursing. Spiritual powers lie behind a blessing and demonic powers behind a curse. I wonder if we've really grasped the kind of authority that comes when we pronounce blessings on God and each other.

Although God is totally self-sufficient and needs nothing from us, he still chooses to receive blessing from us. Something in his heart loves to be 'completed' by our blessing. Moses pronounced a blessing over the Israelites when he said, 'The LORD bless you and keep you' (Num 6:24). If I'm leading worship I'll sometimes ask people to speak that blessing to one another. Some people are rather glib about it, but if you speak it with authority, a real power will be released through it.

Zamar

Literally, to touch the strings (of a harp or lyre). It refers to praising the Lord in song, with harmony and musical accompaniment. David said, 'My heart is steadfast, O God; I will sing and make music with all my soul. Awake, harp and lyre! I will awaken the dawn' (Ps 108:1–2).

Shabach

To congratulate, to speak well of. It suggests triumphantly celebrating, glorying and shouting, as in 'Praise the LORD, all you nations; extol him, all you peoples' (Ps 117:1). The word translated 'extol' is *shabach*.

Samach

To be glad, to rejoice. This word implies an outburst of spontaneous joy which overflows in physical action. Emotion is expressed in singing, dancing and the playing of musical instruments. This sort of worship isn't planned. The worship leader doesn't say, 'Right let's do this'. It just happens. This is one of the characteristics of revival. Everyone suddenly starts singing the same hymn or song all at once. There's a supernatural dimension to it. David says, 'Be glad in the LORD, and rejoice, O righteous, and shout for joy, all you upright in heart!' (Ps 32:11 RSV) *Samach* is also used for the way God spontaneously rejoices over what he's done: 'May the glory of the LORD endure for ever; may the LORD rejoice in his works' (Ps 104:31).

Siys

To be bright, to leap with mirth. David says, 'May all who seek you rejoice and be glad in you' (Ps 40:16). The charismatic hop is very biblical and we need to see more of it in worship. So jump around with all your might!

Giyl

To rejoice, to cry out and be glad. This is another characteristic of revival. Individuals spontaneously shout praises to the Lord. Habakkuk declared, 'I will rejoice in the LORD, I will be joyful in God my Saviour' (Hab 3:18).

Ruah

To raise a shout, a battle cry, a jubilant shout of joy. The psalmist says, 'Come, let us sing for joy to the LORD; let us shout aloud to the Rock of our salvation' (Ps 95:1). When Israel went to war, the leader of the army would raise a battle cry which probably demanded a response from the people. One Old Testament battle cry is, 'For the LORD and for Gideon' (Judg 7:18).

Quara

To call, or proclaim. David says, 'I proclaim righteousness in the great assembly' (Ps 40:9).

Just to complete the 'jewel' I'd like to give you some Greek words for worship in the New Testament.

Proskuneo

This is a very common New Testament word for worship. It means to come towards to kiss. Originally the word had to do with kissing the earth as part of pagan worship, but gradually the idea changed to an inner attitude of heart rather than an outward gesture. It's an expression of intimacy and adoration. Jesus used the word, *proskuneo* when he said, 'God is spirit, and his worshippers must worship in spirit and in truth' (Jn 4:24). It also appears in Matthew 2:2; Luke 4:8 and Revelation 4:10; 19:10 and 22:9.

Sebomai

Originally this word was used to express the idea of shrinking away from the gods out of reverence and fear. Sebomai emphasises feelings of reverence and awe in the presence of

God. The word is used of Titius Justus, who was called 'a worshipper of God' (Acts 18:7).

Latreuo

This word, translated 'worship', appears in Paul's letter to the Philippians: 'For it is we who are the true circumcision, we who worship by the Spirit of God, who glory in Christ Jesus, and who put no confidence in the flesh' (Phil 3:3). Latreuo tells us that worship is not only an inner attitude, but that it's also demonstrated in righteous living. The word appears three times in connection with sacrificial ministry (Rom 9:4; Heb 9:1,6). Paul says, 'Offer your bodies as living sacrifices, holy and pleasing to God — this is your spiritual act of worship' (Rom 12:1). Worship is demonstrated by lifestyle. We live to praise God in whatever we do.

Chaira

To rejoice. This word is most often translated, 'rejoice'. Originally it implied the joy of celebrating at a festival. This joy is expressed and sustained, even through persecution and trial — because the Christian's hope is in Christ. There's a difference between joy, which is a fruit of the Spirit, and happiness, which depends on happenings.

Joy isn't a superficial thing. It's given to us by the Holy Spirit and it stays with us even when were going through terrible trials. Jesus tells us that people will insult, persecute and say all kinds of evil against us because of him. When that happens we must 'Rejoice and be glad' (Mt 5:12). The word he uses here is *chaira*, which is also used in Luke 1:14 and in Philippians 1:4; 2:28,29; 3:1 and 4:10.

Agaillo

To rejoice greatly, to exult, to lift up. This joy is demonstrated in action. The Philippian jailer brought Paul and Silas a meal and 'was filled with joy because he had come to believe in God' (Acts 16:34). The word, agaillo is used here and also in Luke 1:47 and 1 Peter 1:8.

These Hebrew and Greek words give us some insights into biblical worship. I quite often meditate on the words in this list because I want to avoid getting locked into doing the same things when I praise God. I find that they keep me fresh in worship.

Chapter 9

Expressions

of Worship

Cup Final day is written into my diary. Nothing but an emergency interrupts it. I sit there, glued to the TV, watching thousands of football supporters waving their scarves, banners and rattles and listening to their enthusiastic songs and chants. When they roar, I'm right there roaring with them, and when they throw back their heads in despair, I'm doing the same. It's great!

Real enthusiasm is rare in this laid-back, passive generation. Maybe we'll blow up a few balloons and throw some streamers at a royal wedding, general election or New Year celebration. But once the event is over, we'll slump into the armchair and have our passivity restored by a barrage of TV soap operas, quiz shows and advertisements.

To most people, enthusiasm has nothing to do with God. Who could ever be enthusiastic about church, Bible reading or prayer? Yet the word 'enthusiasm' comes from the Greek *enthousiazo* which means 'inspired by' or 'possessed by God'. Just as the word 'Christian' was originally an insulting nickname for a believer in the early church, so in the eighteenth century the word 'enthusiast' became an offensive term for the early Methodists. John and Charles Wesley, George Whitefield and others had a zeal that contrasted with the barren correctness of the established church. They were viewed as dangerous and discredited as 'enthusiasts'.

Jesus wants us to love God with all our heart, soul, mind and strength — with our whole personality and every ounce of our being. If the gospel gives us something to be really excited about, it's sad that Sunday services can be so lifeless. When John Bunyan described the conversion of Christian in *Pilgrim's Progress*, he certainly knew the joy of forgiveness:

> *'Then was Christian glad and lightsome, and said with a merry heart, He hath given my rest by His sorrows, and life by His death. Then he stood still awhile to look and wonder, for it was very surprising to him that the sight of the cross should thus ease him of his burden. He looked again even until the springs that were in his head sent waters down his cheeks. Then Christian gave three leaps for joy, and went on singing.'*

Pilgrim's Progress by John Bunyan, © Hodder and Stoughton.

People who meet with God are 'filled with an inexpressible and glorious joy' (1 Pet 1:8). Surely it's unnatural to suppress Spirit-inspired joy. But do church services give us freedom to express our love to God openly?

The book of Psalms is the Old Testament book of worship and it describes a whole range of human emotion through which we can praise God. If the psalms were used to illustrate worship under the Old Covenant, how much more should they inspire worship under the New? The psalms exhort us to sing, dance, shout, raise our hands, clap, stand up, bow down and speak out. Heart worship expresses itself through the body. It must be demonstrated.

When we're in the New Covenant, we present ourselves as living sacrifices to God and worship him with the whole of our life. But we add a new dimension to our worship when we employ heart, soul, mind and strength in physical praise. We have a relationship with God, he lives in us, we've experienced his love — these things should prompt us to be enthusiastic in our praise. We, of all people, should have a genuine *enthousiazo* experience.

EXPRESSIONS OF WORSHIP

1. CORPORATE SINGING

One of the simplest ways of releasing emotion is through song. A contented baby readily responds to the gentle lullaby of a caring mother. Whether it's a romantic love song or a patriotic national anthem, singing is an integral part of humanity — a gift from a God who himself loves to sing.

Recently the Holy Spirit has been inspiring many new songs, so there's no reason for churches to get stuck in all the old ones. A good Christian song is fairly easy to sing and contains sound doctrine — if not actual words of scripture. These songs can be complemented by great doctrinal hymns like 'The God of Abraham praise', 'Praise my soul the King of heaven', 'Crown him with many crowns' and 'Join all the glorious names'.

Faith comes by hearing the word of God, so when we sing the truth together we'll grow in faith. It's the word, not the song that stirs faith, but when the two go together, the effect can be quite dramatic. Several years ago I was in a prayer meeting when we began singing, 'Blessed be the God and Father of our Lord Jesus Christ.' We sang it over and over for nearly half an hour because God was doing something in people. They were receiving revelation of his fatherhood and were finding new security in his love. The word brought revelation, inspired faith and changed their lives.

Singing can also bring a sense of God's presence. David said, 'Sing to God, sing praises to His name; Cast up a highway for Him who rides through the deserts' (Ps 68:4 NASB). Whenever I lead worship I have the sense that I'm actually making a way through the heavenlies on which people can walk with God. In other words, we praise God, he owns that praise and comes among us.

This is a very controversial idea which is open to misunderstanding. Some people say that if you go through a certain progression of things in worship, God will turn up. You sort of sing yourself into his presence. We must be very careful about this kind of teaching because it doesn't really line up with a biblical understanding of the presence of God.

The Bible tells us that God is present everywhere. David said, 'Where can I go from your Spirit? Where can I flee from your presence? If I go up to the heavens, you are there; if I make my bed in the depths, you are there' (Ps 139:7–8).

Then there's God's realised presence. We consciously realise that he's there and approach him to speak to him. There's no ritual required. Jesus has shed his blood for us and we enter 'by a new and living way' (Heb 10:20) and enjoy fellowship with him.

Finally, there's the manifest presence of God. We know that God has drawn close to us and actually experience a strong sense of his presence. The Israelites encountered the manifest presence of God when Solomon dedicated the temple. The priests took the ark of the covenant into the Most Holy Place, everyone began singing to the Lord and

*'Then the temple of the LORD was filled with a cloud,
and the priests could not perform their service because
of the cloud, for the glory of the LORD filled the temple
of God'* (2 Chron 5:13–14).

Naturally, we must beware of using singing to create an
artificial atmosphere which we take to be God's presence.
God is looking for worshippers — people who will sing truth
from their hearts under the inspiration of the Holy Spirit. He
delights to manifest his presence to a company of worshippers
who are like that.

When Paul and Silas were in prison, they refused to give in
to the pain and difficulty of their situation. Instead, they sang
hymns of praise to God. Their worship time was interrupted
by an earthquake which opened all the prison doors and all
the prisoners' chains. As a result, the jailer was converted
and Paul and Silas were set free (Acts 16:16–34). Of course,
the two apostles weren't praising to create an effect or to
work up some kind of manifestation of God's presence. It
was natural for them to express their love and thanksgiving
— whatever their circumstances.

2. SINGING IN THE SPIRIT

It's hard to find corporate singing in the Spirit mentioned in
the Bible, although there is a reference to singing 'with my
spirit' (1 Cor 14:15). Jesus says, 'in the presence of the
congregation I will sing your praises' (Heb 2:12). John says
that the voice of Jesus is 'like the sound of rushing waters'
(Rev 1:15). I think that's what singing in tongues sounds like.
We, the body of Christ, sing in the Spirit and the sound is
like Jesus singing.

When we sing in tongues, our worship is lifted into an eternal
heavenly realm and God draws very near. Spirit-inspired

worship is about singing songs, shouting our acclamation, bowing in reverence and interspersing these things with spontaneous singing in tongues. The result is a glorious medley, composed not by any musical genius, but by the creative Spirit of God.

3. PROPHETIC SINGING

At David's tabernacle there seems to have been a prophetic singing workshop. Under David's direction, the musicians and singers came together to prophesy in song and with their instruments. Asaph, Heman and Jeduthun directed their families in prophesying, giving thanks and praising the Lord. Singers and instrumentalists were appointed and trained to give a musical lead to the congregation of Israel.

Before Saul became king, Samuel instructed him to go to Gibeah. Samuel said:

> 'As you approach the town, you will meet a procession of prophets coming down from the high place with lyres, tambourines, flutes and harps being played before them, and they will be prophesying' (1 Sam 10:5).

So here we see music, instruments and singing all being associated with prophesying. Isaiah sang one of his prophecies. The Bible says, 'I will sing for the one I love a song about his vineyard' (Is 5:1). Habakkuk 3:1 says, 'a prayer of Habakkuk the prophet. On *shigionoth*.' That term *shigionoth* was a musical term which meant that the prophecy was probably sung.

So prophecies can be sung as well as spoken. Music helps to communicate words and when the Spirit is inspiring both words and music, there can be a great openness to what God is saying. I've often been in meetings where singing in the Spirit has been followed by a prophetic song. On one occasion, the congregation sang about the Father glorifying his name in the earth and went into a time of singing in tongues. Out of this came a prophetic song exhorting us to be merciful, compassionate and kind so that God's glory would be revealed in our lives. This prophecy was further underlined by the preaching which followed.

4. PROPHETIC PLAYING

Not only is there a place for prophetic singing, there's also a place for prophetic playing. We read, 'Whenever the spirit from God came upon Saul, David would take his harp and play. Then relief would come to Saul; he would feel better, and the evil spirit would leave him' (1 Sam 16:23). Elisha prophesied to the music of a harp:

> 'While the harpist was playing, the hand of the LORD came upon Elisha and he said, "This is what the LORD says ..."' (2 Kings 3:15).

I witnessed something similar a few years ago at a worship conference in DeBron, Holland. At that conference were pastors, elders, worship leaders and musicians from all over Europe and each nationality was sitting together. I was leading worship with Graham Kendrick. One evening Graham taught his song based on Psalm 133 with the chorus that goes, 'Join our hearts together in love'. While the congregation was singing the song, there was a space for the instruments to play and the oboist walked up to me. He told me that he felt that God had given him some insight into the people and said that he wanted to play a lament over the congregation. This was to express the sorrow over what the nations had done to one another during the Second World War.

While he was playing the oboe, the hand of the Lord came upon the congregation and melted the hearts of the people. The French began to reach out to the Germans, and the Germans to the Dutch. Individuals were praying for one another and there were tears of repentance. The whole dynamic of the meeting changed as God broke down the dividing walls between the nations.

On another occasion I was leading a worship celebration in Singapore. I took a friend called James with me to play percussion in the worship band. The band was very competent but didn't know much about prophetic playing and improvising. As we led the worship I became rather concerned because I felt that the people were just singing the songs. I wondered if they were simply inhibited or thought that they'd come to a concert. I was struggling and longing for a greater depth of worship in the congregation. After we'd sung several songs, I felt prompted to read from Revelation 19. I began reading:

> *'I saw heaven standing open and there before me was a white horse, whose rider is called Faithful and True. With justice he judges and makes war ...'*

As I went on, James began to cut loose with a percussion solo, interpreting what I was saying on the drums. I read:

> *'His eyes are like blazing fire, and on his head are many crowns ... He treads the winepress of the fury of the wrath of God Almighty.'*

By that time the drums were resounding and the cymbals crashing. As the reading developed and the solo built in its intensity, individuals began to leap out of their seats with their hands in the air. I invited people to come forward for prayer. Many fell over under the power of the Spirit, some were healed and some were given prophetic words. It was a remarkable time.

At one Stoneleigh Bible Week a woman gave a prophecy about the state of the nation. She spoke with deep feeling about the terrible godlessness and rebellion in the UK and expressed the pain in God's heart. As she was prophesying, the cellist in the band began playing a lament for the nation. At the end of the prophecy, a spirit of prayer swept across the people who were moved to cry out to God for revival.

5. INSTRUMENTAL ACCOMPANIMENT

Psalm 150 exhorts us to praise the Lord with all kinds of instruments and many of the psalms give directions about accompaniment. For example, Psalm 81 has the direction, 'For the director of music according to *gittith*' — which was probably the forerunner to the guitar. The Psalm starts:

> *'Sing for joy to God our strength; shout aloud to the God of Jacob! Begin the music, strike the tambourine, play the melodious harp and lyre.'*

These were the instruments that could be used to accompany this Psalm.

Musical accompaniment can often interpret the words of a song and help the congregation to worship. The right drum beat can lift our spirits and get us dancing. The more melancholy sound of a cello or oboe can touch our hearts and make us receptive to the Holy Spirit. The strident tones of the brass can stir us to rejoice in Jesus' victory. And the trumpet can remind us of God ascending with a shout.

Some people have a problem with instrumental solos. They think that it's somehow not right to listen to music without words. But God creates beautiful sunsets, mountains, landscapes, flowers, trees, birds and animals simply for us to enjoy. He inspires music and can inspire the creative musician to play a beautiful melody or harmony and stir us to appreciate his creativity.

The God who is constantly surrounded by music and enjoys it uses music to draw us into worshipping him. So let's not be afraid of instrumental music. Certainly there's always the danger of showing off, but that could also be said of preachers who use clever words to impress their congregations.

In this current move of the Holy Spirit, it's very helpful to have solo singing during ministry times. A gentle solo voice singing songs like, 'Let your living water', or 'Come Holy Spirit' can set the right atmosphere for ministry and prayer. The sensitive playing of instruments during this time can also be very beneficial.

6. ANTIPHONAL SINGING

Some congregations were divided into two groups to sing certain psalms. Each group sang a phrase in turn. Psalm 136 was probably sung in this way. Group 1 would sing, 'Give thanks to the LORD, for he is good,' and Group 2 would respond, 'His love endures for ever.'

7. RESPONSIVE SINGING

Some psalms require a response from the congregation. Take Psalm 98 for example. One of David's directors of singing may have declared the first three verses beginning, 'Sing to the LORD a new song'. Then the congregation would have responded, 'Shout for joy to the LORD, all the earth.' These exhortations would have been meaningless unless they'd met with the appropriate response. When the director declared, 'Make music to the LORD with the harp, with the harp and the sound of singing' the harpists and singers would have played and sung. When he said, 'with trumpets and the blast of the ram's horn' the trumpeters and horn players would have joined in. And when he said, 'shout for joy before the LORD, the King' the congregation would have shouted. So the Psalm was more than a poem to be read, it was a means of expressing praise. As the director of singing exhorted, the orchestra and congregation responded.

8. RAISING HANDS

A small child stretches his hands up to a parent for a cuddle or to attract attention. There's a simplicity and a deep trust in his action. Similarly, hand raising is a very simple means of expressing love to God and surrender to him. It also helps us to release any inhibitions. I think that hand raising is one of the most neglected actions in worship — we've become almost blasé about it. By raising our hands we're making a prophetic statement to the principalities and powers that Jesus is Lord. We raise our hands to:

Bless the Lord — *'Lift up your hands to the sanctuary, And bless the LORD' (Ps 134:2 NASB).*

Dedicate ourselves — *'May my prayer be set before you like incense; may the lifting up of my hands be like the evening sacrifice' (Ps 141:2).*

Express desire — *'I spread out my hands to you; my soul thirsts for you like a parched land' (Ps 143:6).*

Intercede — *'I want men everywhere to lift up holy hands in prayer' (1 Tim 2:8).*

9. CLAPPING HANDS

In Scripture, clapping has to do with applauding the king. At a coronation the new monarch was acclaimed with shouts and applause. Clapping was also a sign of rejoicing — although it wasn't connected with clapping to the beat. Psalm 47:1 exhorts us, 'Clap your hands, all you nations' and Psalm 98:8 declares, 'Let the rivers clap their hands.'

10. DANCING

This is controversial in worship because of its immediate visual impact and the danger of sensuality. Like all creative gifts, dance is neither moral nor immoral. It's how we use movement that brings it into the moral realm.

God created dance and loves to participate in it. Zephaniah said, 'The LORD your God is with you ... he will rejoice over you with singing' (Zeph 3:17). The Hebrew word for rejoice here is *gil*, which means to spin around in delirious delight as a result of great emotion. If God is with us and rejoicing over us with dancing, shouldn't we join in and dance with him? The Bible gives three reasons for dancing.

It releases joy

Psalm 150:4 says, 'Praise him with tambourine and dancing'. Miriam danced over the defeat of the Egyptians (Ex 15:20) and David leapt and danced before the Lord (2 Sam 6:16). When Jeremiah prophesied restoration for Israel, he described it as a time of great rejoicing, 'Again you will take up your tambourines and go out to dance with the joyful' (Jer 31:4). Real joy needs physical expression. When the lame man was healed, he didn't worry what the religious authorities in the temple thought about his actions. God had met him, so he leaped for joy.

It expresses community

Jeremiah was referring to the New Covenant people when he said, 'Then maidens will dance and be glad, young men and old as well' (Jer 31:13). The Hebrew word for dance here is *mecholah*, which means a communal or round dance. Many cultures express their community life by dancing together. Kingdom people could do the same — dancing to demonstrate their togetherness. It's easy to devise simple steps to current songs for parents and children to follow.

It interprets truth

It isn't just music that can enhance words, movement can do the same. Providing there are safeguards against sensuality, a solo dancer or group of dancers can minister pure worship to God by his Spirit.

The week after Keith Green was killed in a plane crash, I attended a meeting where a Christian professional dancer danced to a record of Keith singing Psalm 23. She interpreted in movement the confidence that we have in entering the valley of the shadow of death. It was very moving. On another occasion, I was at Spring Harvest. As the band played Chris Bowater's song, 'Lamb of God', I spoke about repentance, forgiveness and wearing the robes of righteousness. This was totally unrehearsed. While I was speaking about freedom in Christ, a girl came up and acted like someone who was bound up. Then another girl danced across the platform and draped a white robe across the first girl. Their spontaneous dance really reinforced the truth.

Dramatic mime is often used to convey truth. Ezekiel mimed the exile of the Israelites (Ezek 12:3–7). A woman anointed Jesus' feet with her tears and with ointment, and wiped them with her hair (Lk 7:36–50). Agabus acted out a prophecy when he took Paul's belt and bound his own hands and feet with it (Acts 21:10–11).

11. BOWING

The first Commandment says, 'You shall have no other gods before me' (Ex 20:3). Bowing implies submitting to, revering and worshipping something. God tells us that one day 'all mankind will come and bow down before me' (Is 66:23). The physical act of bowing, kneeling or lying prostrate reminds us of the time when every knee will bow to Jesus (Phil 2:10). If we love God, we won't feel forced to bow. We'll freely respond to his grace with submissive hearts.

12. SHOUTING

There's a time for silence in worship, and a time for shouting. Let's not be frightened of either. Silence doesn't need to be awkward, nor does shouting need to be an empty noise. The psalmist exhorts us, 'Shout for joy to the Lord, all the earth' (Ps 100:1).

God wants us to worship him with every part of our being — spirit, mind, will, emotions and body. A time of worship should never be a spectator activity. How can we be passive when we come together to worship God? Surely he wants us to participate fully in physical praise — singing, raising our hands, clapping, dancing, bowing and shouting — because we're so enthusiastic about him.

to the PRAISE
of his GLORY

When Jesus asked the disciples, 'who do people say the Son of Man is?' they replied, 'Some say John the Baptist; others say Elijah; and still others, Jeremiah or one of the prophets'. When Jesus asked them, 'Who do you say I am?', Peter replied, 'You are the Christ, the Son of the living God.' And Jesus said to him, 'Blessed are you, Simon son of Jonah, for this was not revealed to you by man, but by my Father in heaven' (Mt 16:13–17).

Christianity is God-initiated and God-revealed — which is what makes is different from other religions. Knowing God's character — his will, workings and ways — comes only by revelation. God reveals himself in his word and this must be the basis for everything that we believe about God. We can worship him according to our own ideas. We must learn to worship him according to the Scriptures.

The current worship scene abounds with interesting vocabulary: 'prophetic worship', 'creative worship', 'lifestyle worship', 'worship warfare' and many others. These aren't necessarily wrong. I use them myself because I want to see every area of worship recovered. The problem is that each one touches only one facet of truth and if we're not careful, we can become limited by them. Or we can use them as novelty expressions which we think might help to get us out of our boredom with 'ordinary worship'.

Many people think that they can make worship more interesting by being a bit more creative. 'The young people will worship better if we do it this way,' they think. But worship doesn't emerge from novelty ways of presentation. It flows from an understanding of truth. When we know what God has done for us in Christ, we'll express heartfelt worship to him. Then it won't matter whether we're singing a gentle worship song, or a great hymn. It won't matter whether we're standing listening to a resonant pipe organ, or leaping with joy to an enthusiastic band. Once the truth grips us, it will lead us into exciting expressions of worship.

Worship is essentially about our relationship with God. The shorter Westminster Catechism states, 'The chief end of man is to glorify God and enjoy him for ever.' Worship is our response to our relationship with God. This relationship is based on revelation — the revelation that God is our Father, that his Son is our Redeemer and that the Spirit is his indwelling presence. The more we understand the truth about the greatness of our salvation, the better our worship will be.

All Scripture is inspired and there are some sections of it that particularly unlock our understanding. This is true of Ephesians 1:3–14 which explains why God created us and the wonder of our relationship with him. We can divide this passage into three parts: verses 3–6, 7–12 and 13–14. Each of these sections ends with a similar phrase: 'to the praise of his glorious grace' (v. 6), 'for the praise of his glory' (v. 12) and 'to the praise of his glory' (v. 14).

We're here to live to the praise of God's glory. God has given us many reasons to praise him, but he isn't a detached person, a tyrant who demands our obedience. He's a loving Father who longs to have a close relationship with us. That's why he wants to help us with anything that prevents us from knowing him better and enjoying his presence more. I want to look at Ephesians 1 more closely because I know that once you've grasped the truths in it, they'll release you in worship.

EPHESIANS 1:3-6

Ephesians 1 begins with an exhortation to praise God. Commenting on this, Dr Martyn Lloyd-Jones says:

> 'But let us note that the praise and the adoration and the worship are to be ascribed to the blessed Holy Trinity. "Blessed be the God and Father of our Lord Jesus Christ, who hath blessed us with all spiritual blessings." The blessings come through the Holy Spirit. The praise and worship and adoration, indeed all worship, must be offered and ascribed to the Three blessed Persons. The Apostle Paul never fails to do this. He delights in mentioning the Father and the Son and the Holy Spirit. The Christian position is always and inevitably Trinitarian. Christian worship must be Trinitarian if it is true worship; there is no question, no choice about this. If we have the correct biblical view of salvation, then the Three Persons of the blessed Holy Trinity must always and invariably be present ...

> 'Not only must we be careful always that the Three Persons are in our minds and our worship, we must be equally careful about the order in which they are introduced to us in the Scriptures — the Father, the Son, the Holy Spirit. There is, what our forefathers called a divine economy or order in the matter of our

salvation among the blessed Persons themselves; and so we have always to preserve this order. We are to worship the Father through the Son by the Holy Spirit. Many evangelical Christians in particular seem to offer all their prayers to the Son, there are others who forget the Son altogether, but two wrongs do not make one right. So we notice here at the commencement of this Epistle that the Apostle not only praises, but praises the three blessed Persons and ascribes unto them thanksgiving and glory in this invariable order ...

'Thus we begin to see why Paul says, "the God and Father of our Lord Jesus Christ'. God before time, and before the world, saw our predicament and entered into this agreement with His own Son. He has taken an oath, He has signed, He has pledged Himself in a covenant, He has committed Himself. Everything is in Christ. He is our Representative, He is our mediator, He is our Guarantor — all blessing comes in and through Him. Who can realize what all this meant to the Father, what all this meant to the Son, what all this meant to the Holy Spirit? But that is the gospel and it is only as we understand something of these things that we shall begin to praise God.'

God's Ultimate Purpose, D. M. Lloyd-Jones, © 1978 D. M. Lloyd-Jones, the Banner of Truth Trust. Used by permission.

These verses explain the Father's part in your salvation. They tell you that God has blessed you with every spiritual blessing in Christ, that he chose you before he made the world, that you have a goal — to be holy and blameless, that God calls you his very own child and that he has adopted you into his family, the church. God is totally committed to you. You'll never encounter a more radical truth than this: God loves you unconditionally and eternally.

How could Paul and Silas sing praises to God in their prison cell? How could the early church martyrs worship as they went to their deaths in the Roman arena? This is how: they understood God's love for them. Grasp how much God loves you and you'll have incredible security. Then you'll be able to worship God confidently whatever happens to you.

Vic Morley was a good friend of mine. He'd been involved with Church of Christ the King, Brighton since it began in 1978 and many church members were grateful for his loving practical support. In 1993 he joined a work party and went to one of the townships in South Africa where he helped to build houses. He was a very fit man and had no hint of serious illness until January 1994 when he began to get problems swallowing. At first the doctor thought it was indigestion, then suggested that it might be an ulcer. But Vic actually had very severe cancer of the oesophagus which required immediate surgery.

His family was naturally very concerned for him and he asked the church elders to anoint him with oil and pray. As we did this, we asked God to heal him and release him from any anxiety concerning the future. Over the next few days I continued to pray for his healing and also for God's presence to be with him in a powerful way. Then, one Saturday I found myself praying in song. The tune came quickly and I sang it over and over again. The words went:

In every circumstance of life
You are with me glorious Father
And I have put my trust in you
That I may know the glorious hope to which I'm called
And by the power that works in me
You've raised me up and set me free

And now in every circumstance
I'll prove your love without a doubt
Your joy shall be my strength.

The following day, I taught the song to the congregation at the Sunday morning meeting. Vic and his family were there and I somehow felt that it would mean something very special to them. A short time later, Vic went to be with the Lord. We sang the song at his funeral.

Praise isn't based on happenings. The circumstances of life shouldn't govern how we feel or what we think. We don't worship God from a superficial earthly perspective, but because he's worthy of our praise. He's created us for future glory and we're bound to experience difficulty and pain while we're here on earth.

Certainly, God does heal the sick, but not everybody gets healed. Some of the most wonderful testimonies I've heard have come from people who've proved God's faithfulness in the most severe trials. They've refused to let their faith be shaken because they've been gripped by the truth that God is their Father. They know that he's with them, that he loves them and that he's constantly watching over their lives.

God made you to know, love and serve him. He's in control of your life. His word says that 'in all things God works for the good of those who love him' (Rom 8:28). If you know that he's sovereign, you won't go round with the attitude, 'Well, hallelujah anyway'. You'll be certain that God is your fortress and your strength, your confidence in life or death.

He'll be your joy in sickness, in sorrow, in suffering, in unemployment — in every circumstance of life. You'll know that your Creator Father God is with you, working out his purposes in and through you, preparing you for glory. Once you understand these things, they'll stir you to sing to the praise of his glorious grace.

EPHESIANS 1:7–12

These verses tell us what Jesus has done to reconcile us to God. In the Old Testament God said, 'The soul who sins is the one who will die' (Ezek 18:4). God is holy and sin separates us from him. Jesus shed his blood for our sins so that we could be reconciled to the Father. When we accept Christ's sacrifice on our behalf, God gives us free access to himself and forgives us for all our sins. He pours his grace into our lives, gives us all wisdom and understanding and reveals his great eternal plans to us.

Many people have a problem with the idea that Jesus has reconciled them to the Father. That's because of their earthly experience of fatherhood. While others have had good fathers, their fathers have been absent, uncommunicative, abusive, harsh or weak. And their relationship with their father, or lack of it, has deeply affected their personality.

I'm grateful that I had a wonderful earthly father. From my early childhood he taught me how to pray, read my Bible and preach. He spent time with me, told me fascinating stories, introduced me to music, encouraged and affirmed me. I'm so thankful to him, but there still came a point where I needed a revelation of God as my Father which went beyond my understanding of earthly fatherhood.

What we need to realise is that our understanding of God's fatherhood has nothing to do with whether we had a good, bad or absent earthly father. We're all on the same level because we all need to know God as our Father in a personal

141

way. The knowledge of God's fatherhood comes by revelation through his Son. Jesus said, 'No-one comes to the Father except through me' (Jn 14:6). And Fanny Crosby underlined this truth in the words of her timeless hymn:

> *O Come to the Father through Jesus, the Son;*
> *And give Him the glory — great things he hath done.*

We have three basic needs: identity, security and self worth. Originally God wanted our parents to build these things into us, but that hasn't always happened. Today family life has broken down and parents have failed to fulfil God's plan, with the result that there are many hurting people in society. Feelings of rejection, insecurity and lack of self worth can dominate our lives and stop us from enjoying the presence of God. So how do we get free from them? We go to Jesus and see how he related with his Father and how he refused to yield to these sorts of negative feelings. And we discover afresh exactly what he did for us when he reconciled us to God.

When Jesus was on earth, he needed his Father to establish his identity, security and self worth. After he was baptised, the Spirit came down on him and God said to him, 'You are my Son, whom I love; with you I am well pleased' (Lk 3:22). Later, God reinforced this truth when he said to the disciples on the Mount of Transfiguration, 'This is my Son, whom I have chosen; listen to him' (Lk 9:35). On both occasions he was reminding Jesus of who he was, telling him that he was loved and confirming that he was valuable.

We sometimes forget that Jesus was a human being. If he was 'tempted in every way, just as we are' (Heb 4:15), he must have known what it was like to face the temptation, 'You're no one special. God doesn't love you. You're insignificant.' Indeed, he had several encounters with the

Pharisees about his identity. They said that he was a Samaritan and demon-possessed (Jn 8:48), that he wasn't from God (Jn 9:16) and that he was raving mad (Jn 10:19). They even questioned who had fathered him (Jn 10:33). These challenges must have hit Jesus hard and tempted him to yield to feelings of rejection. I wonder if it's significant that when he left his accusers he 'went back across the Jordan to the place where John had been baptising in the early days' (Jn 10:40). Could it have been that he simply wanted to return to the place where his Father had confirmed his identity?

One of the biggest problems that we face is rejection. Its roots lie in a lack of parental love with the result that the heart is conditioned to feelings of rejection. There are several causes of rejection.

First, there's rejection in the womb. A pregnant woman who doesn't want to have a baby may reject it before it's born and may consider, or even attempt to have an abortion. As the child grows up, he may have severe relationship problems. I've prayed through this kind of rejection with several people and they've experienced a wonderful release.

Second, there's what we might call sibling rejection, which is a classic family problem. When a second child is born, the first one may become jealous of the attention that the new baby is getting from his parents. This can result in brothers and sisters comparing themselves unhelpfully and rivalling one another.

Third, there's rejection by those in authority. This can happen at school where a child isn't fully accepted by a teacher or an authority figure. When I was in my fourth year at school I was doing subjects that didn't appeal to my temperament. The teachers should have tried to help me, but they often ridiculed me instead. In one woodwork lesson I was mocked by a teacher because I couldn't get my piece of wood planed square. This resulted in my developing a terrible fear of going into the woodwork lesson. I also began having behavioural problems because I didn't feel that I was being valued.

Fourth, there's peer group rejection. Children can be very cruel to one another. The only child in the class with glasses, or with a brace on his teeth may become a target for rejection by the rest. Similarly, if one person in a group of teenagers isn't allowed to stay out late, he's likely to be ridiculed and to feel rejected.

Fifth, there's parental rejection, which is the worst of all. A father or mother who has a tendency towards perfectionism can't accept what the child does because it's never perfect enough. Sometimes parents find it hard to express love to their children. This can be particularly true of fathers who are too busy to communicate. Parental rejection can condition someone to feel, 'I'm not loved' and can cause all kinds of emotional traumas. It can lead to self-rejection and even to thoughts of, or attempts at suicide.

Sixth, there's rejection of others. When people try to express love to us, we resist them by putting up barriers, wearing masks and refusing to show our feelings. There's a conflict inside. We want to be loved and enjoy deep relationships, but our fear of rejection forces us to keep others at a distance.

Feelings of rejection can affect our relationship with God. We become conditioned to rejection, to fearing rejection, to rejecting others and to self rejection and we project that rejection onto God. But if we're 'in Christ', what God says to Jesus, he says also to us. This means that the words, 'You are my Son, whom I love; with you I am well pleased' apply to you and me just as much as they did to Jesus. If we continue to yield to feelings of rejection we slip into unbelief and are effectively saying, 'I don't believe that what God says about me is true'.

We must understand the power of the cross. When Jesus reconciled us to God, he didn't just deal with the penalty of our sin, but also with the power of sin over our lives. Isaiah says, 'the punishment that brought us peace was upon him' (Is 53:5). The word, 'peace' here means 'emotional well being'. Jesus has taken on himself all our rejection, pain and hurt. The cross makes us emotionally whole.

Have you ever thought that Jesus went through every possible human rejection? We may romanticise the Christmas story, but how did Mary's parents and friends really react to her when they discovered that she was pregnant? She must have told them about the angel, about the Holy Spirit overshadowing her, and about having a baby without sexual relations. But did they really believe it all? Mary wouldn't have rejected the baby in her womb, but many of her relatives and friends probably did — since it was a disgrace for an unmarried woman to have a child.

Jesus went through sibling rejection. He had brothers and sisters (Mt 13:56) and his brothers 'did not believe in him' (Jn 7:5). He was rejected by his peers. Judas betrayed him with a kiss, Peter denied him and all the other disciples fled when he needed them most. Then there was parental rejection. Jesus cried out from the cross, 'My God, my God, why have you forsaken me?' That was the ultimate rejection.

All our pains, our feelings of isolation, our feelings of not being loved, our feelings of having no value — all those questions about our identity are poured out on Jesus at the cross. Paul makes such a powerful statement when he says, 'We have redemption through his blood, the forgiveness of sins'. It's amazing what God has done for us in Christ. Jesus sacrificed his life to the Father, and the Father's wrath against sin was poured out on him.

So if you want to know something of the Father's love, you need to see that Jesus has dealt with everything that's separated you from God. He died to free you from your rebellious sinful nature and also from the devastating effect of sin on your life. Now he wants you to know his love and his inner peace and harmony. He wants you to throw off anything that prevents you from enjoying your relationship with him.

Jesus has been raised from the dead and you are seated with him in heavenly places (Eph 2:6). It makes a difference to you when you know you've been reconciled to God, that you've been forgiven, that God is planning your future, that all your hurts have been dealt with at the cross and that your identity is in Christ. Once you really grasp the Father's love through Jesus, you can't help worshipping and living for the praise of his glory.

EPHESIANS 1:13–14

The Father initiates our salvation and the Son accomplishes it through his death and resurrection. Now Paul tells us what the Holy Spirit does:

> 'Having believed, you were marked in him with a seal, the promised Holy Spirit, who is a deposit guaranteeing our inheritance until the redemption of those who are God's possession — to the praise of his glory' (Eph 1:13).

The Holy Spirit is described as a seal, and a seal does two things. First, it authenticates. A seal on an official document guarantees what's written in it. Second, it establishes ownership. In the days of the Wild West an animal was branded to show who owned it. The Holy Spirit is also described as a deposit. The Greek word translated, 'deposit' is *arabon* which means a down payment guaranteeing a finished payment which is in kind.

I'll illustrate this. In Bible times people used to trade with animals. Let's say that I've got ten camels and want to buy a hundred sheep. I ride one of my camels to the sheep trader and we strike up a deal: ten camels for a hundred sheep. Now I've only come with one camel — the one I'm riding, so I put that down as an arabon, a down payment. When I get home, I discover that one of my camels has died. It's no good my returning with eight camels and four goats hoping that the sheep trader will accept them. I've deposited a camel and have to pay in kind. So I must find another camel from somewhere to complete the deal.

The kingdom of God is past present and future. When God fills us with his Spirit he takes something of this eternal kingdom and puts it in us as a down payment which guarantees our future inheritance. As Fanny Crosby puts it in her hymn:

> *Blessèd assurance, Jesus is mine!*
> *O what a foretaste of glory divine!*

Salvation is more than being delivered from sin and reconciled to the Father. God has sealed us with his Spirit and brought us into the dimension of the Spirit. We're no longer merely human, God lives in us and we see through spiritual eyes. When we read the word, the Holy Spirit brings it alive. He gives us the power to prophesy, do exploits of faith, give words of knowledge, discern spirits, pray for the sick, witness and preach. As we meditate on great truths about the fatherhood of God and redemption in Christ, the Holy Spirit wells up within us as stirs us in our worship. No longer are we governed by our emotions and circumstances. We live from the life source of the Spirit.

True worship is trinitarian. We come to Jesus, he restores us to the Father and the Holy Spirit writes everything into us — he seals us. When we're baptised in the Spirit, we have more than an intellectual knowledge that God is our Father. The Spirit within us cries, 'Abba, Father' (Rom 8:15) and 'Abba' is a term of loving intimacy used by a child of his father. Worship is wrapped up in relationship: we love God, obey him and live to the praise of his glory. The more we understand of God's character and the way he works, the more we will worship him.

Worship ministry must flow from worshipping hearts. We can lead people only as far as our own experience of God. As one verse of the old hymn by Ruth Tracy goes,

> *Only as I truly know Thee*
> *Can I make Thee truly known;*
> *Only bring the power to others*
> *Which in my own life is shown.*
> *Show Thy power in me,*
> *That I may be used for others;*
> *Show Thy power in me.*

True worshippers know that their security is in God. They can sing with confidence, 'He is my fortress. I will never be shaken' and worship flows naturally from their lives. God wants us all to be living like this — set free by truth and experiencing the power of the Holy Spirit. When we worship in Spirit and in truth, we will serve effectively and enjoy the blessing of God. There won't be any conflict between preaching, worshipping, serving and social action. The preaching will teach people how to mature in Christ. The worship will give them the opportunity for corporate praise and thanksgiving. And practical acts of kindness and social action will bring glory to God. Love for him will motivate our evangelism, prayer meetings and counselling programmes — indeed, everything we do.

That's the ideal, but why do we — as individuals and corporately — fall so far short of it? Because the devil uses a variety of tactics to stop us from being worshippers and they all hinge on a misunderstanding of what God has done for us in Christ.

HINDRANCES TO WORSHIP

We've already looked at the problem of rejection. If we question, 'Does God really love me?' we haven't understood that his love is unconditional. Feelings of rejection may have their roots in childhood hurts or in a sense of devaluation by people in authority. When we project these hurts onto God, we're sinning because we're refusing to believe what he says about us. A bondage to rejection will affect our worship because we'll doubt whether God will receive what we express to him.

Rejection can also affect a worship ministry team. This happens when individuals create relationship tensions by projecting their deep rooted feelings onto one another. Symptoms of rejection will include unhelpful comparisons with others, lack of self-worth, perfectionism, negative criticism and self-protection. If the problem is extreme the individuals concerned should seek prayerful support.

The worship leader or minister and musicians need to be able to draw the congregation into a deep appreciation of God's unconditional love. Paul said:

> *'I am convinced that neither death nor life, neither angels nor demons, neither the present nor the future, nor any powers, neither height nor depth, nor anything else in all creation, will be able to separate us from the love of God that is in Christ Jesus our Lord'* (Rom 8:38–39).

Let's believe this and make sure that we totally reject the feeling, 'I'm not accepted.'

Condemnation also stops us from living to the praise of God's glory. Paul says:

> *'There is now no condemnation for those who are in Christ Jesus, because through Christ Jesus the law of the Spirit of life set me free from the law of sin and death'* (Rom 8:1–2).

Condemnation is about imprisonment and we're no longer imprisoned, we're in Christ. God has totally forgiven and acquitted us. We've been justified. It's just as if I'd never sinned. We're not struggling with two natures. The old one is crucified with Christ and the new one is completely righteous. Paul says:

> *'You ... are controlled not by the sinful nature but by the Spirit, if the Spirit of God lives in you'* (Rom 8:9).

We're in an unshakeable position and have no reason to wallow in condemnation. Certainly, confession is important, but it mustn't emerge from condemnation or come at the beginning of a worship time. The Lord's Prayer begins, 'Our Father in heaven' and continues much later, 'forgive us our debts'. Confession of sin at the beginning of a prayer or worship time will create a negative effect. Worship begins with God, not us.

God wants us to approach his throne and worship him with confidence (Heb 10:19–20). The writer to the Hebrews says:

> 'Let us draw near to God with a sincere heart in full assurance of faith, having our hearts sprinkled to cleanse us from a guilty conscience and having our bodies washed with pure water. Let us hold unswervingly to the hope we profess'
> (Heb 10:22–23).

Worship leaders, musicians and congregation must learn to focus on God and declare his praise on the basis of what Jesus has done. We should never stand consumed by a feeling of unworthiness — which is actually a sign of unbelief. If we open our hearts in worship, God will lovingly convict us of anything that needs putting right.

Super-spirituality is another hindrance to worship. We become super-spiritual when we try to add spiritual values to disobedience. For example, a worship leader can think that praise and worship will release God's presence in a meeting. But the mechanics of praise and worship will achieve nothing if that individual isn't living uprightly before God. Amos recognised this problem when he prophesied against religious externalism. He said:

> 'I hate, I despise your religious feasts; I cannot stand your assemblies. Even though you bring me burnt offerings and grain offerings, I will not accept them. Though you bring choice fellowship offerings, I will have no regard for them. Away with the noise of your songs! I will not listen to the music of your harps. But let justice roll on like a river, righteousness like a never-failing stream!' (Amos 5:21–24)

Inner integrity is more important than external expression. God is more interested in purity and righteousness than in beauty and creativity.

We overcome these hindrances by going back to basics. Whatever style our worship services take, we must remember that worship is fundamentally about our relationship with God. The true worshippers worship in Spirit and in truth.

When will we live to the praise of his glory? When we understand who we are in Christ, when we are secure in our relationship with the Father and when we're filled with the power of the Holy Spirit. Our understanding of these things will affect the way we work, the way we relate to one another and the decisions we make. It will affect our desire to read God's word, to witness and to communicate the gospel. It will stop our Christian service from becoming cold and formal and change our motivation from duty to love.

The truth affects our lives. It sets us free. God wants to see a company of people who know this freedom on an individual basis — because this will affect our corporate worship. When we come together to sing our praises, pray, prophesy and preach there'll be a credibility and integrity about us. A knowledge of our identity in Christ will make our public testimony ring true.

The truth of who we are in Christ is beautifully expressed in Charitie Lees Bancroft's great hymn:

Before the throne of God above
I have a strong, a perfect plea;
A great High Priest, Whose name is Love,
Who ever lives and pleads for me.

My name is graven on His hands,
My name is written on His heart;
I know that while in heaven He stands
No tongue can bid me thence depart.

When Satan tempts me to despair,
And tells me of the guilt within,
Upward I look, and see Him there
Who made an end of all my sin.

Because the sinless Saviour died,
My sinful soul is counted free;
For God, the Just, is satisfied
To look on Him and pardon me.

Behold Him there! the risen Lamb!
My perfect, spotless, Righteousness,
The great unchangeable I AM,
The King of glory and of grace!

One with Himself, I cannot die;
My soul is purchased by His blood;
My life is hid with Christ on high,
With Christ, my Saviour and my God.

CHAPTER 11

HOW *to be a* WORSHIPPER

C an you actually worship God while you're leading people from the front?' People often ask me that. Maybe they feel a tension between the mechanics of worship — such as playing an instrument — and the pouring out of your heart to God. I don't see any conflict between them. I'm convinced that if we're true worshippers, we can enjoy the presence of God wherever we are and whatever we're doing.

I can remember the first time I skied a black run — the speed and sheer exhilaration. Maybe fear gripped me, I don't know, but I suddenly found myself singing in tongues at the top of my voice as I hurtled down the mountain. I couldn't help giving glory to God in what I was doing.

Worship is about offering our bodies as living sacrifices to God (Rom 12:1). If we're always conscious of him, we won't slip into worship mode when we arrive at a Sunday meeting, we'll come already worshipping. Certainly, I feel that it's very important to prepare our hearts before we go to any meeting — to be ready to give as well as receive. But we need to learn how to live for God's glory every moment of every day. So if you want to be a worshipper, you must focus first on your relationship with God. Tozer said:

> *'I am of the opinion that we should not be concerned about working for God until we have learned the meaning and the delight of worshipping Him. A worshipper can work with eternal quality in his work.'*

> Whatever Happened to Worship? by A. W. Tozer, © Christian Publications Inc. 1985, published in the UK by OM Publishing, Carlisle.

The problem is that in our modern world, there's so much to distract us and it isn't easy to fix our minds on the Lord. We forget that he's always with us, that we can talk freely to him, thank him, praise him and draw on his grace in times of temptation. If we remembered these things, they'd help us to keep God at the centre of our lives and encourage us to develop a consistent relationship with him.

Moses summed up the law to the Israelites when he said:

> *'And now, O Israel, what does the LORD your God ask of you but to fear the LORD your God, to walk in all his ways, to love him, to serve the LORD your God with all your heart and with all your soul, and to observe the LORD's commands and decrees that I am giving you today for your own good?' (Deut 10:12–13)*

These verses actually embrace the whole of New Covenant life. Jesus referred to them when he said, that the most important command was this:

> *'Love the Lord your God with all your heart and with all your soul and with all your mind and with all your strength' (Mk 12:30).*

FEAR THE LORD

First, Moses said that the Israelites should fear the Lord. This doesn't mean that we should be afraid in a negative sort of way. It means that we should live in awe of him and have a constant awareness that he's there. This needs practice because we often spend too much time reading the newspaper or watching the television. When I was a child, my father used to prepare on Saturday night for the various Sunday meetings. He'd clean all the shoes and get everything ready. We never had Sunday newspapers — not because Dad was legalistic, but because he didn't want anything to distract his mind before he went to the house of God.

I've tried to follow his example — particularly in this recent move of the Spirit. I don't want to crowd my mind with things before a worship time, so I avoid too many social engagements on Saturday nights and spend the time thinking and praying about the Sunday meetings. I try to go to bed early. On Sunday I'm tempted to read about the Saturday sport, but I don't do that because I don't want to be preoccupied with issues that might divert my attention from God. This isn't a legalistic thing. I don't think it's wrong to be interested in the sport's results or to read the Sunday newspaper. It's just that I want to go to the worship time with my mind focused on God and ready to worship. I know that we enter into God's presence by grace, but I fear him and want to please him — so I try to discipline myself.

God is awesome. John Arnott came from Toronto to England to speak at a conference in Brighton and I was leading worship. One morning the sense of God's presence was unbelievable. We'd had a couple of prophetic words and had been singing about the glory of God, when you could almost say, 'the cloud just seemed to descend on us.' Some people were prostrate, others were kneeling or bowing. There were physical manifestations too. As I stood there on the platform I remembered the time when David was bringing the ark back to Jerusalem. I recalled how Uzzah reached out to steady it and how God struck him down. Suddenly I didn't want to touch the ark — to take the meeting anywhere when God was so clearly in control. I had a healthy fear of starting another song, and for a long time we just worshipped in silence.

The fear of the Lord helps us to obey him. The Bible says, 'The fear of the LORD is the beginning of wisdom' (Prov 9:10). It's wise to know that he's always with us, that he gives us every breath, hears every word that we speak, knows every thought we think and sees every attitude in our hearts. Surely, these things should encourage us to fear him.

WALK IN ALL HIS WAYS

All of life's activities should be to the praise of God's glory — that's what walking in his ways is all about. Paul tells us to 'walk by the Spirit' (Gal 5:16, NASB). The word translated, 'walk' comes from the Greek verb, *peripateo* from which we get peripatetic. When I taught music we had several peripatetic music teachers who went from one school to another. Paul wants us to be peripatetic in the Spirit — everywhere we go we're living with a consciousness of God's presence.

Paul underlines this idea when he exhorts us to 'be filled with the Spirit' (Eph 5:18). The tense of the verb here suggests constant filling. Certainly, God will refresh us when we've been pouring out our lives for him, but he wants us to be engrossed in the Spirit all the time. A few years ago Rosie and I decided to take up mountain biking to keep fit. I didn't know anything about mountain bikes so I started going into mountain bike shops, buying mountain bike magazines, reading articles and watching TV programmes about mountain bikes. I almost became obsessed. I was familiar with every kind of mountain bike that there was, and knew all about gears, frames and forks. I had all this knowledge, but I still didn't buy any bikes. One day, Rosie declared — almost in desperation, 'The trouble is with you is that you're filled with mountain bikes.' I was preoccupied with them. And God wants us to be preoccupied with the Spirit.

In Galatians 5:25, Paul tells us to 'keep in step with the Spirit'. The Greek verb here is *stoicheo*, which means to walk in a line — in other words, to follow the inner promptings of the Holy Spirit. We need to check what we feel the Spirit is saying against the word of God, because the Spirit never contradicts the word. It's also wise to chat to a more mature Christian about a proposed course of action. If we follow inner conviction, confirmation from the Scriptures and input from mature Christians, we'll keep in step with the Spirit. I think that it's also important to keep in step with one another — so there's a relationship challenge too.

LOVE HIM

Love is at the heart of the gospel. It's God's love that causes him to reveal himself to us. The verse that gospel preachers probably quote more than any other is John 3:16:

> *'For God so loved the world that he gave his one and only Son, that whoever believes in him shall not perish but have eternal life.'*

Although God hates sin, he still extends his love to the sinner. When we become Christians, the Holy Spirit reveals God's love to us — not just in our heads, but in our emotions. He prompts us to declare with enthusiasm:

> *'How great is the love the Father has lavished on us,
> that we should be called children of God! And that is
> what we are!' (1 Jn 3:1)*

God's love is everlasting, a love that will not let us go, a love
that's been born in eternity and will last for ever. Even when
we sin and stray from God, he still loves us. His discipline
isn't a sign of his hatred, but of his love:

> *'My son, do not make light of the Lord's discipline, and
> do not lose heart when he rebukes you, because the
> Lord disciplines those he loves, and he punishes
> everyone he accepts as a son' (Heb 12:5–6).*

If God's love for us is that great, we should be motivated
both to 'keep [ourselves] in God's love' (Jude 21) and to
express our love to him. Paul prayed, 'May the Lord direct
your hearts into God's love' (2 Thess 3:5).

Loving words and actions will sustain romance and keep a
marriage alive. True love needs to be communicated. God
has communicated his love to us through his word. He's
touched our emotions by pouring out his love on us by his
Spirit. And he's proved his love in action by answering our
prayers and working out his purpose in our lives. We need to
respond to this love. The Song of Songs reveals the love
between the bride and bridegroom. The first few verses are
full of passion, intimacy and romance:

> *'Let him kiss me with the kisses of his mouth — for your
> love is more delightful than wine. Pleasing is the
> fragrance of your perfumes; your name is like perfume
> poured out' (Song 1:2–3).*

Our worship shouldn't only be based on objective truth, but
on passionate and extravagant expressions of intimacy to the

Lord. To sing, 'Jesu, lover of my soul, let me to thy bosom fly' is a wonderful expression of intimate desire. But the depth of emotion can easily be lost in its familiarity and antiquated language. Perhaps we need to use everyday language in our worship. Paul says:

> *'I pray that you, being rooted and established in love, may have power, together with all the saints, to grasp how wide and long and high and deep is the love of Christ, and to know this love that surpasses knowledge — that you may be filled to the measure of all the fulness of God' (Eph 3:17–19).*

SERVE HIM

We often say that people are 'serving God' if they've fulfilled a ministry in a particular place or are in involved in some public aspect of church life. But we mustn't see serving God as something done by the chosen few. We're all called to active service rather than passivity in the pew!

Service is the natural outflow of love for God and it's about action. We fulfil God's will on earth by serving him in the context of the world and the church. Paul exhorted the slaves in Ephesus to obey their masters. He said:

> *'Serve wholeheartedly, as if you were serving the Lord, not men, because you know that the Lord will reward everyone for whatever good he does, whether he is slave or free' (Eph 6:7–8).*

As we go through the round of life's activities, our attitude should be, 'I'm living before God and everything I do is serving him.' This will affect the way we drive our car, do our work, treat our wife or husband and relate with our children.

Our attitude to people in the world will also reveal whether we're serving God. Homelessness and social deprivation are serious problems in modern society, especially in large towns and cities. Some people do 'sponge off the state' and some can use aggressive intimidating tactics, but they have little hope of escape — and they're living under our noses.

One day I was walking along a Brighton street when a young man approached me and asked me for some money so that he could catch a bus to another part of town. I immediately thought, 'How cheeky' said, 'No' and walked on. After a few minutes I had an overwhelming sense of conviction. God said, 'How do you know that I didn't send him to you so that you could help him? How do you know that he wasn't an angel in disguise?' Suddenly I realised that a true worshipper has a generous, serving heart. I also decided that I needed closer moment by moment fellowship with the Spirit, so that I could look for opportunities to serve God through practical acts of kindness. If we enjoy fellowship with the Spirit, he will teach us to discern between the genuinely needy and the 'spongers'.

A heart which loves God will overflow with love to others and look for ways to serve them. A truly worshipping church will have a programme of social action which expresses its service to God. It will remember the words of James:

> 'Religion that God our Father accepts as pure and faultless is this: to look after orphans and widows in their distress and to keep oneself from being polluted by the world' (Jas 1:27).

And it will remember the words of Jesus:

> 'For I was hungry and you gave me something to eat, I was thirsty and you gave me something to drink, I was

> *a stranger and you invited me in, I needed clothes and*
> *you clothed me, I was sick and you looked after me, I*
> *was in prison and you came to visit me. Then the*
> *righteous will answer him, "Lord, when did we see you*
> *hungry and feed you, or thirsty and give you something*
> *to drink? When did we see you a stranger and invite*
> *you in, or needing clothes and clothe you? When did*
> *we see you sick or in prison and go to visit you?" The*
> *King will reply, "I tell you the truth, whatever you did*
> *for one of the least of these brothers of mine, you did*
> *for me"' (Mt 25:35–40).*

We need to work out our worshipping lifestyle with others in the church. The church is the body of Christ and we're individually members of it. Each part is significant and vital to the health of the whole. Many tasks need to be done to help church life run smoothly. We need overhead projector operators, P.A. people, stewards, children's workers, cleaners, those who give hospitality and maintain the building. A preacher can spend hours preparing to preach, but he can't function if nobody's there to open the building, steward the people, or care for the children. We should do these tasks lovingly and joyfully — as if we were serving the Lord, not men.

OBSERVE HIS COMMANDS AND DECREES

Not only should our love for God motivate us to serve, it will also motivate us to obey. If we say, 'I love God' and then ignore the clear commands of Scripture, we court spiritual disaster. Saul learnt about this. The prophet Samuel commanded him to destroy the Amalekites, but he only partially obeyed. He spared King Agag and the best of the cattle and sheep. Saul then added to his disobedience by trying to deceive Samuel. He claimed that he'd obeyed Samuel's instructions, when he hadn't. Samuel, who could hear the

bleating of the sheep and the lowing of the cattle, challenged
Saul over his disobedience and Saul tried to justify himself
by saying that he was going to sacrifice the animals to the
Lord. In other words, he tried to cover his disobedience with
an act of worship. Samuel replied:

> 'Does the LORD delight in burnt offerings and sacrifices
> as much as in obeying the voice of the LORD? To obey is
> better than sacrifice' (1 Sam 15:22).

We must beware of allowing the externals of worship — the
music, the hand raising, the singing and dancing — to be
superimposed on disobedience to God's word. True
worshippers don't go through external motions. They obey
God. Jesus said:

> 'If anyone loves me, he will obey my teaching. My
> Father will love him, and we will come to him and
> make our home with him' (Jn 14:23).

HEART, SOUL, MIND AND STRENGTH

We express our worship to God by loving him with all our
heart, soul, mind and strength — every moment of our lives.
We worship him with our hearts and souls by being passionate
about him. We worship him with our minds by reading
Scripture, meditating on it, reading books and commentaries
about it. And we worship him with our strength by serving
him and using our bodies both in our public meetings and
private times of praise. Psalm 119 is a wonderful Psalm for
people who want to be worshippers. David said:

> 'I have hidden your word in my heart that I might not
> sin against you. Praise be to you, O LORD; teach me
> your decrees' (Ps 119:11–12).

First, he used his mind to meditate on God's word, then he spoke out of what was in his heart:

> 'With my lips I recount all the laws that come from your mouth. I rejoice in following your statutes as one rejoices in great riches' (Ps 119:13–14).

I think that we've lost the art of contemplation — maybe because it conjures up the idea of monasteries. But there's something about coming simply to enjoy the Lord, to gaze on his beauty and meditate on some aspect of his character. We need to set time aside to do that.

Today we've got some very helpful aids to worship — devotional books like *The Pleasures of God* by John Piper, and worship albums. I'll often play a worship album and sing along to it. And sometimes I'll feed my spirit by playing one track over and over again. The music that we listen to doesn't have to come from a worship album. I enjoy all kinds of music — classical, rock, jazz and even brass bands. I listen to it for its own sake, but I can also worship God through it because I believe that he created music for the blessing and benefit of mankind.

Worship through creation

We often spend lots of time thanking God for what he's done for us through Jesus, but we can praise him in other ways too. Many of the psalms magnify God for his creativity. We read, 'The heavens declare the glory of God; the skies proclaim the work of his hands' (Ps 19:1). Psalm 104:1–15 particularly exalts God as Creator.

> 'O LORD my God, you are very great;
> you are clothed with splendour and majesty.
> He wraps himself in light as with a garment;

he stretches out the heavens like a tent
and lays the beams of his upper chambers on their
waters.
He makes the clouds his chariot and rides on the wings
of the wind.
He makes his messengers, flames of fire his servants.

He set the earth on its foundations; it can never be
moved.
You covered it with the deep as with a garment;
the waters stood above the mountains.
But at your rebuke the waters fled,
at the sound of your thunder they took to flight;
they flowed over the mountains,
they went down into the valleys,
to the place you assigned for them.
You set a boundary they cannot cross;
never again will they cover the earth.

He makes springs pour water into the ravines;
it flows between the mountains.
They give water to all the beasts of the field;
the wild donkeys quench their thirst.
The birds of the air nest by the waters;
they sing among the branches.
He waters the mountains from his upper chambers;
the earth is satisfied by the fruit of his work.
He makes grass grow for the cattle,
and plants for man to cultivate —
bringing forth food from the earth:
wine that gladdens the heart of man,
oil to make his face shine,
and bread that sustains his heart.'

When we wake up in the morning and look out of the window,
let's be grateful for what's out there. Let's thank God for the

sunshine, the rain, the thunder, the wind, and the birds in the trees. When we go on a walk in the country or on a stroll by the sea, let's worship him for the flowers, the animals and the sunset. Let's praise him for our food too. Paul exhorts us to give thanks to God for everything (Eph 5:20). The world around us serves to remind us of the greatness of God as Creator and sustainer of everything.

WORSHIP THROUGH INTIMACY

Worship is also expressed through intimate fellowship with Jesus. This is best illustrated by the story of Mary. She

> *'took about a pint of pure nard, an expensive perfume; she poured it on Jesus' feet and wiped his feet with her hair. And the house was filled with the fragrance of the perfume' (Jn 12:3).*

Judas objected to her action on the grounds that the perfume should have been sold and the money given to the poor. But Jesus commended Mary and said, 'It was intended that she should save this perfume for the day of my burial.' Let's look briefly at the quality of Mary's worship.

It was motivated by love and gratitude. She was thankful to Jesus for what he had done for her. It was also extravagant. She wasn't afraid to express her emotion by weeping in front of others. She was the sort of person who wouldn't have been embarrassed to raise her hands, shake and fall on the floor. She just wanted to give herself to the Lord Jesus. Her worship was costly too. The perfume was expensive and she could have sold it or kept it for herself. But she chose to pour it over Jesus' feet instead.

Mary's worship was personal. It's an intimate thing to be seen wiping someone's feet with your hair. The Song of Songs tells us about the relationship between the beloved and his lover. It begins, 'Let him kiss me with the kisses of his mouth — for your love is more delightful than wine' (Song 1:2). There's an intimacy between the Bridegroom and the bride — Jesus and his church. Finally, Mary's worship was a prophetic statement pointing to Jesus' death.

This worship didn't embarrass Jesus. On the contrary, it had his total approval because it was the sort of worship that he wanted to receive.

WORSHIP THROUGH COMMUNITY

It isn't enough to be worshippers on our own, we also need to be worshippers among other people. Together we're God's church, and 'church' is an Anglo-Saxon translation of the Greek word, *ecclesia* which means 'to be called out for a purpose'. We've been called out and gathered for a purpose — primarily to worship God. We don't go to church, we are the church and our gatherings give us visibility and identity.

The idea of gathering is rooted in the Old Testament. Moses assembled the Israelites at the Passover and the people continued to meet together for special occasions when they were wandering in the wilderness. The focal point of these gatherings was the Tabernacle. Later, the people gathered at the Tabernacle of David. At their feasts they celebrated what God had done for them and looked forward to future blessings. The New Testament church also gathered together.

Why did the people gather? To meet with God. They experienced his presence in the Old Testament, but in a greater way in the New. You only have to skim through the book of Acts to see the power of God at work in the gathered church. People were full of awe, signs and wonders abounded, unbelievers were saved and sin was judged. Either you were totally committed to this community, or you stayed away because God's presence made you afraid.

When I was a child I used to love visiting my grandmother's house. That wasn't because of the journey, the house itself or even the treats I could expect. It was because my grandmother was there. God wants us to love the place where he lives.

> *'How lovely is your dwelling-place, O Lord Almighty!*
> *My soul yearns, even faints, for the courts of the Lord'*
> (Ps 84:1).

> *'I rejoiced with those who said to me, "Let us go to the*
> *house of the Lord"'* (Ps 122:1).

Let's not neglect gathering together. Together, we're the temple of God and he wants to manifest himself among us. Peter says:

> *'As you come to him, the living Stone — rejected by*
> *men and chosen by God and precious to him — you*
> *also, like living stones, are being built into a spiritual*
> *house to be a holy priesthood, offering spiritual*
> *sacrifices acceptable to God through Jesus Christ. For*
> *in Scripture it says:*

> *"See, I lay a stone in Zion,*
> *a chosen and precious cornerstone,*
> *and the one who trusts in him*
> *will never be put to shame."*

> *Now to you who believe, this stone is precious. But to*
> *those who do not believe,*

> *"The stone the builders rejected has become the*
> *capstone,"*

and

*"A stone that causes men to stumble
and a rock that makes them fall."*

*They stumble because they disobey the message —
which is also what they were destined for. But you are a
chosen people, a royal priesthood, a holy nation, a
people belonging to God, that you may declare the
praises of him who called you out of darkness into his
wonderful light' (1 Pet 2:4–9).*

Peter begins, 'As you come to him.' The sense here is that
we keep coming — it's an habitual thing. It's also worth noting
that we come primarily to Jesus, not to one another. Jesus
said that the true worshippers worship in Spirit and in truth.
The Greek word for 'worship' here is *proskuneo* which means
'to come towards, to kiss'. So every time we gather to worship
we should expect to be intimate with Jesus.

Jesus' invites us to come even when we're weary and heavy
laden, because he gives us rest (Mt 11:28). I feel sad when
people don't come to meetings because they're tired, feel a
bit unwell, or are having a hard time. They may think that
they need space, but they really need to be among God's
people. Jesus didn't say, 'If you're weary, stay at home' but
'come to me.' He also invites the thirsty to 'come to me and
drink' (Jn 7:37). We're in a season of the outpouring of God's
Spirit and he wants us to drink deeply. Let's do that.

When Peter describes Jesus as the 'living Stone', he's thinking
about God's dwelling place. When the disciples remarked
on the beauty of the stones in the Temple, Jesus replied, 'the
time will come when not one stone will be left on another;
every one of them will be thrown down' (Lk 21:6).

He was pointing to the day when God would build a spiritual temple and when he would be its living cornerstone. David knew that the house of God was the best place to be in all the earth. He said:

> *'One thing I ask of the LORD, this is what I seek: that I may dwell in the house of the LORD all the days of my life, to gaze upon the beauty the LORD and to seek him in his temple' (Ps 27:4).*

The world doesn't see the church as God's building, or Jesus as the chief cornerstone. But we do. We don't come to meetings legalistically because we're expecting to meet Jesus. We have the same attitude as Evan Roberts who once said that he was scared to miss a meeting in case revival broke out at it.

Our reaction to the living Stone determines whether we're Christians or not. Peter says that the living Stone is 'rejected by men.' There's no such thing as a nominal Christian. Church going will save no one. The point is, are we coming to the living Stone or rejecting him? This passage in 1 Peter describes someone who's rejecting Jesus. It gives four symptoms of rejection:

The first symptom is shame. Peter says, 'The one who trusts in him will never be put to shame'. Sin causes guilt and shame, so the person who doesn't trust in Jesus will be ashamed to meet him. But if we trust in Jesus, he takes away our shame.

The second and third symptoms are stumbling and falling. Peter says that Jesus is 'A stone that causes men to stumble and a rock that makes them fall.' Sin imprisons people. We fall into it and become enslaved to habits, fears, depression, anxiety and lust.

The fourth symptom is disobedience. Peter says, 'They stumble because they disobey the message.' We sin when we break God's Law and he holds us responsible for this.

The human race is divided into two: those who come to the living Stone and those who reject him. Jesus is rejected by men, but he's 'chosen by God and precious to him.' If we understand God's attitude to Jesus, it will affect our worship because what's precious to God will be precious to us as well.

There's something tremendous about being a parent. My father once told me that he didn't realise how much his father loved him until he had me. And I didn't understand how much my father loved me until my first son was born. If this is true on a human level, how much more true is it in the relationship between the Father and Jesus? I wonder if the angels had been rehearsing for ages to sing to the newborn king, but only a few shepherds were around to hear them. The Father was celebrating his Son's birth. When Jesus was twelve years old, he was going about his Father's business. At his baptism and on the Mount of Transfiguration the Father called him his beloved Son. And when Jesus performed miracles, he was doing what the Father had told him to do.

Jesus is precious to God and he should also be precious to us. Peter says, 'to you who believe, this stone is precious.' Knowing that Jesus is precious is an important key to worship. I often hear people giving their testimonies and it saddens me when they say things like, 'I prayed and it felt good' or 'I'm happy now that I know God' or 'I've had peace of mind since I became a Christian' or 'Someone laid hands on me and I shook.' These things may well be true, but we must put worship into our testimonies.

Jesus is precious because he died to save us, because he rose from the dead to give us new life, because he's now exalted in heaven, because he's always interceding for us and because one day he'll return and take us to be with him. We must never lose the wonder of our salvation, or fail to declare it to others.

Peter says that we 'like living stones, are being built into a spiritual house.' Each individual is important, but we're also placed into a relationship with others. Paul says:

> *'In him the whole building is joined together and rises to become a holy temple in the Lord'* (Eph 2:21).

The Authorised Version translates this better when it says that we're 'fitly framed together' which brings in the idea that we've been bonded together and chosen to live harmoniously. Christ is the living Stone, the Spirit joins us together and the building grows through relationship and action. At the heart of this community is worship. We've been called so that we may declare God's praises — as individuals and with others.

CALLED TO BE WORSHIPPERS

God wants the whole of your life to be an expression of worship to him. Every morning when you get up, be filled with praise and gratitude to God. Every day set aside times when you stop and thank him that he's saved you, that he loves you and that Jesus is coming back for you. Every night when you go to bed think about God's goodness, his faithfulness, his mercy and compassion. If you dwell on these things, they'll motivate and inspire you in your relationship with him and they'll bolster your faith when you face trials and pressures during the day.

You'll develop as a worshipper as you learn to fear the Lord, walk in all his ways, love him, serve him and obey him, and as you worship him in creation, with intimacy and among his people. This hymn of Charles Wesley sums up personal worship. I'll leave it with you.

Talk with me Lord: Thyself reveal,
While here o'er earth I rove;
Speak to my heart, and let it feel
The kindling of Thy love:

With Thee conversing, I forget
All time, and toil, and care;
Labour is rest, and pain is sweet,
If Thou, my God, art here.

Here then, my God, vouchsafe to stay,
And make my heart rejoice;
My bounding heart shall own Thy sway,
And echo to Thy voice.

Thou callest me to seek Thy face,
'Tis all I wish to seek,
To attend the whispers of Thy grace,
And hear Thee inly speak.

Let this my every hour employ,
Till I Thy glory see,
Enter into my Master's joy,
And find my heaven in Thee.

to those
WHO LEAD

A master conductor commented to a trainee, 'All your clever theatrical movements may look good on the podium, but if you can't make the orchestra play in time, then you might as well not be there.' The goal of a good conductor is not to draw attention to himself, but to get the very best out of an orchestra. So a good worship leader isn't there to perform for the people, but to stand before them and guide them in their worship.

Where do you find worship leaders in the New Testament? What's the main goal in worship leading? What do you do if a worship time is going flat? How do you choose which songs to sing? What part do children play in worship? What do you do about people who are hurting? Many Christians are keen to know the answers to these sorts of questions. I want to answer them here. Even if you're not a worship leader or musician, I think that you'll benefit from this chapter because it should give you a better understanding of the dynamics of worship.

Where do you find worship leaders in the New Testament?

You don't! But Paul could easily have had this ministry in mind when he said, 'If a man's gift is ... leadership, let him govern diligently' (Rom 12:6,8). The Greek word translated, 'leadership' comes from a verb which means 'to stand before'. Paul also referred to 'gifts of administration' (1 Cor 12:28). An administrator is a kind of helmsman, and a worship leader is an administrator in that he or she steers a meeting in a particular direction.

What's the main goal in worship leading?

It's to cast up a highway so that God's presence can be manifested among his people. You can't contrive this. All you can do is pray and allow the Holy Spirit to lead the meeting in such a way that it actually happens. People have often encountered this tangible sense of God's presence in revival. But it's not limited to revival. God is sovereign and will manifest his presence whenever and wherever he likes.

Several years ago I was teaching on the Christian life to about twenty or thirty young people at a youth camp at Pyecombe. One evening we were all sitting in a circle in the marquee drinking hot chocolate and praying when the Spirit suddenly fell on one of the girls. From then until about 3.00am the Spirit just kept coming down on people. Two young people called Jane and Christine were standing next to each other. When the Spirit came on Jane, she started speaking in tongues. Christine didn't believe in this gift but recognised the language as Greek because she was doing A Level Greek at the time. Many other things like this were happening, and one guy was converted. The amazing thing was that immediately you walked out of that field, you lost the sense of God's presence. And when you walked into it again, the sense of God's presence returned.

We need to experience more of this dimension of worship and the manifest presence of God before we pray for people in our meetings. We can get into our intercessions and petitions much too soon and pray without first touching the heart of God. Praise and worship should open the door to prayer. When Solomon's Temple was completed, the Israelites worshipped, the presence of God came, Solomon prayed and then God answered.

What's the most important quality of a worship leader?

The best worship leaders are worshippers. They're constantly filled with the Holy Spirit and live each day under his direction. I'd encourage all worship leaders to spend lots of time meditating on the Scriptures, worshipping and praying. Then, when they stand at the front to lead worship, they'll minister to others out of their experience of God during the week.

What characteristics do you look for in worship musicians?

I think that the principles in 1 Samuel 16:17–18 are very helpful here. Saul was tormented by a demon and wanted a musician to minister to him. One of his servants said:

> 'I have seen a son of Jesse of Bethlehem who knows how to play the harp. He is a brave man and a warrior. He speaks well and is a fine-looking man. And the LORD is with him.'

In our church, people often say that they can play a musical instrument and ask if they can join the worship team. It's always good to have people who are willing to serve like this, but we must consider more than musical gifting. I'd look for musicians with the characteristics mentioned in this verse.

First, David knew how to play the harp. One version of the Bible says that he was a 'skillful musician' (NASB). The desire to sing or play mustn't outweigh skill. The church is the only place I know where you can stand up in front of a crowd, sing or play badly and get away with it — because people are sympathetic towards you. But surely God wants something far better than this.

Worship musicians must have particular musical skills. It isn't enough to be able to read music and perform solos. You need to be able to work with others and blend your music in with theirs. Can you play in a wide variety of keys and flow from one song to another? Are you bogged down by the written music or can you hear other chords and melodies? Can you accompany prophetic singing? I'd look for someone with a basic musical gift who's prepared to develop that gift rather than remain static.

Second, David was a brave man and a warrior. Worship musicians should be confident in God because they have to face particular pressures. The devil doesn't like worship, so you're often vulnerable to criticism, rejection, pride, or feelings of, 'Did I do it well? Was I good enough?' It's important that you're living a victorious Christian life.

Third, David spoke well. Your speech betrays your attitude and it doesn't help to be negative and critical towards others in the band when you're meant to be developing teamwork. You need to be encouraging and positive to others and to honour their gifts

Fourth, David was a fine-looking man. Worship musicians must have an inner confidence about themselves. They aren't self-confident, because their confidence is in God, but they see themselves as he sees them. This is important because you're bound to make mistakes now and again. When you play wrong notes or start something in the wrong key, you mustn't let it preoccupy you. If you're concerned about your self-image and are continually thinking, 'What will people think of me?' you'll never flow in worship.

The worship band in my local church practise hard and like to get their arrangements right, but sometimes we'll play something that we haven't rehearsed. This happened in a recent worship time. I was leading worship and there was a prophecy which prompted me to introduce the song, 'There is a king in Zion, the city of our God.' The musicians didn't know it, but they soon picked it up and the congregation really enjoyed singing it. You have to be quite secure in yourself to be able to do that kind of thing. Musicians must be able to balance skill, rehearsal and practice with spontaneity. They must also remember that they're not performing, but leading people into the presence of God.

I also believe that worship musicians need to be anointed by God's Spirit and set apart for their ministry. Before David entered Saul's service, he was anointed by Samuel. And the musical Levites didn't drift into their work, they were set apart for it. Worship musicians are in a very public place in the church and have a big influence on what happens in the meetings. They need recognition for this.

How do you prepare to lead worship?

Times of worship rarely just happen. Certainly, you should always make room for spontaneity, but there should also be a framework for worship. God is a God of order and the psalms, or worship songs, have structure and shape. If you're a worship leader, you must prepare your heart, develop your skills and be ready for every worship time. If you do these things, the congregation will feel secure in your leadership.

It's important to remember that worship leading isn't so much a matter of preparing songs as preparing yourself — and that's done best in your private times with God. What he says to you in the secret place will have repercussions in the public meeting. If I know that I'm going to lead worship, I pray most about a key song — which usually has a strong worship content. I sing it, meditate on it and get it into my spirit. Why? Because I know that if God has spoken to me through it I can often lead the congregation into the same kind of experience that I've had.

What makes people secure in worship?

I think that people feel secure when they see that you're confident in God and are leading with humility. That means you've got to know your surroundings and the abilities of your congregation. If you give them vague or impossible instructions, they'll find it hard to do what you say. For example, it's no good exhorting them to march around the room singing an unknown song, or encouraging them to dance if there's virtually no leg room. But if you give simple instructions, they'll willingly respond.

What about background preparation?

It's important to have a thorough knowledge of worship songs and popular hymns. It will help if you compile a loose-leaf folder with a flexible indexing system. Then you can record each song with its key signature and file it under a particular heading — praise songs, kingdom songs, testimony songs, warfare songs, songs about God's character — that sort of thing. You could include a scripture reference for each song to undergird the truths that the song is declaring. It's a good idea to prepare a list of song groupings on a particular theme. If you have this information readily available, you'll probably never be taken unawares in a meeting.

How important is communication with the band?

The worship leader must be a good communicator because worship can take an unexpected turn and the musicians can feel very vulnerable. Before the meeting begins, you need to let them know of anything unusual that may happen so that they can be prepared. They won't be blessed if, in the middle of the meeting, you start singing a long-forgotten obscure chorus to which no one has the music.

Be sure to devise a means of communication with the band. I use simple hand signals to indicate whether I want to repeat the whole song, the final verse, or the last line. If you're using an overhead projector, you need to make sure that the acetates you need are there and that the OHP operator knows which songs you want to sing and in which order. This may seem all very mundane, but it's essential if you want things to run smoothly.

How do you come to a worship meeting?

Always with a sense of great expectation that something's going to happen. If you come apologetically, you won't inspire much confidence in the people. But if you let them know that they're going to meet with God, the effect should be quite dynamic.

Is there a special way of approaching God in worship?

No. We don't have to do anything special to get into the presence of God because we always have access to him through the blood of Jesus. However, there are principles in Scripture which help us to know how to approach God. He's holy and we must remember this and come to him with a sense of awe. We must also be careful not to focus initially on our needs. David declared, 'Let God arise, let His enemies be scattered.' It's not until much later that he added, 'Blessed be the Lord, who daily bears our burden' (Ps 68:1,19 NASB).

Should we expect to see the prophetic, priestly and kingly dimensions in all our worship times?

Yes. There should be times when we're declaring truths about God, times when we're offering our sacrifices of praise, and times when we're challenging Satan's rule by taking authority over him in the name of Jesus. We need to be aware of the songs that express these different dimensions and know which dimension we're in at any given moment in a meeting.

What do you do if a worship time is going flat?

This isn't always the fault of the worship leader, musicians or congregation. It just happens. Don't urge the people on or condemn them. You may be able to get them to sing, dance and shout, but they probably won't be worshipping from their hearts. It's better to draw them rather than drive them. The best thing to do is introduce some scripture or songs which express truth about Jesus. If you capture their imaginations, they'll lift their hearts to God in adoration.

How do you avoid panicking?

It's easy to panic. Someone starts up a song that you haven't practised, or you don't know what to do next. That sort of thing can actually make you retreat inwardly. You think you've blown it and then start wondering what the church leaders are thinking. I think you've got to be secure in God and not allow it to get to you. The fact is that you're living to the praise of God's glory and it's what he thinks that's important.

So be relaxed. If you're on edge and constantly wondering what to do next, you're likely to keep jumping in with comments and participating too much. Then the flow of the meeting will become stilted and the people will feel insecure. Simple seed-thoughts should be sufficient to lead people into praise. If someone's read a scripture, try to respond to it. If that scripture is descriptive, the band could even play along while it's being read. For example, the passage about Jesus on the lake could be illustrated by music suggesting wind and waves. But don't be frightened of silence. If the meeting goes quiet, don't think you've got to make something happen. Stand back from it, wait and see what God is doing.

A few years ago I stood on a mountainside in north Wales and watched a buzzard take off from a tree. It rose higher and higher until it was a tiny speck in the sky. I marvelled at the way it rode the thermals and hardly ever flapped its wings. As I watched God said to me, 'That's what should happen in a worship time.'

The important thing isn't to pack in as many contributions as possible, but to ride with the Spirit. Contributions should flow in harmony and create a sense of unity. But just as a sudden gust of wind can affect the flight of a bird, so the unexpected move of the Spirit can change the course of a meeting. So learn to be sensitive to the Spirit and once you discover what he's doing in the meeting, stay with it until he does something else.

How do you choose which songs to sing?

Worship should be in Spirit and in truth. That's why I don't like sentimental worship songs that really don't say much. I choose songs that state truth from the Scriptures because I know that they'll help people to worship. When they sing truth, they'll focus their minds on truth, their minds will feed their spirits and the result will be praise. I believe that every worship time needs to say something about God's character, Jesus and his ministry and the Holy Spirit — because we worship the Father through the Son by the Spirit. I may introduce songs that say other things, but these three elements will always be there somewhere.

What about prophetic singing?

If you're going to sing out prophetic truth, be aware of your vocal limitations. You can start off well but can get so excited that your voice is straining to reach unreachable notes. The content might be there, but the music isn't. If you minister in prophetic song, practise by singing Scripture.

Prophetic singing often needs pruning. After the first couple of sentences it can move on in a directionless or repetitive fashion. To prevent this, understand the gist of the song before you sing and try to form phrases in your mind before you verbalise them. Why not get rid of jargon type words and express yourself in everyday language? You're more likely to keep the interest of the congregation if you do that.

Be careful not to get into a prophetic song to bide time in worship — because you're not sure what to do next. I've done that and most worship leaders can identify with it. If a prophetic song is timely and anointed, it can bring worshippers into revelation and release. It's a significant ministry and if you're involved in it, you need to learn how to wait on God and develop your singing technique so you can give full expression to the truths that you want to convey.

Is there a place for hymns in modern worship?

I believe that our hymnology is an important part of our spiritual heritage. Many of our great hymns are full of doctrine in a form that can be remembered. They express in poetry the greatness and attributes of God. Our contemporary worship songs often lack this depth and for that reason, are popular for a relatively short time. This doesn't make them less important. It's just that a worship song frequently focuses on one aspect of truth while a hymn may develop a doctrine through five or six verses. A good example of this is the hymn, 'Join all the glorious names', which builds up a picture of Jesus as our prophet, priest and king and ends with a great statement of faith.

The problem with singing hymns is that they tend to be culturally irrelevant to the unchurched. People today don't necessarily communicate with that kind of musical form and poetic imagery. But hymns still have an important place and I'd encourage song-writers to study their content and to use them in their own private worship. I'd also encourage the integration of hymns with contemporary worship songs.

You must, however, look at each hymn carefully because the harmonic and melodic structure of a hymn doesn't always allow it to be played in a contemporary way. I have no problems about singing hymns with the accompaniment and in the musical form in which they were written. So don't make these hymns contemporary. Do them, but do them well.

How do you use hymns?

Some hymns do lend themselves to more contemporary arrangements and the tunes can often be re-written. The great revival hymn, 'O God of burning, cleansing flame' by William Booth has a tune which is of little contemporary relevance today. It came alive when Lex Loizides gave it a rock style. I've recently re-written the hymn, 'Breathe on me, breath of God' by Edwin Hatch. I've made the tune very lyrical, but because it's still gentle it's in keeping with the original style. It's a wonderful song to sing in this move of the Spirit.

You can rearrange some hymns by adjusting the harmony. For instance:

> *My heart and voice I raise*
> *To sing Messiah's praise*

goes very well with a contemporary rhythm and can build through each verse. Many contemporary song writers are writing more hymn-like songs. The song 'Great is the darkness' by Noel Richards and Gerald Coates is a contemporary hymn. So there is a place for using hymns and you can express them in a contemporary way.

If you place a great hymn alongside a contemporary worship song, you can also create a good effect. We took the hymn, 'A stronghold sure our God is still' by Martin Luther and sang it in four-part harmony to the organ sound on the synthesiser with the Bach chorale arrangement. Then we went straight into Noel Richards', 'He is our fortress, we will never be shaken'. We were expressing the same truth as the old hymn — there was just a natural transition from one to the other. Musicians need to learn to be creative in the way they use hymns. Sometimes the recovery of a lost hymnology can uncover a wealth of hidden truth.

What part do children play in worship?

Children are natural worshippers. David said, 'From the lips of children and infants you have ordained praise' and then went on to talk about deliverance from enemies (Ps 8:2). So God loves to hear children praising him. One problem is that little children can't read the OHP or understand the words of the songs. Should we exclude them — bearing in mind that many adults find it hard to relate to children's worship — or include them?

Some churches have family services where adults and children can worship together. Ishmael has a gift for involving everyone in worship and has written a number of songs that speak to both adults and children. There's mileage in this, but I think children also need to have their own worship times.

I don't think that we have a high enough spiritual expectation of children, and we don't realise how much they can take in. We forget that Jesus said, 'Unless you change and become like little children, you will never enter the kingdom of heaven' (Mt 18:3). Children can challenge adults by their vulnerability and openness to God.

Our children join us for the first twenty minutes of the main meeting and we try to include them in our worship — not by making it childish, but by involving them in some way. The first two or three songs are often easy for them to understand — 'Father God, I wonder' is a great favourite. One worship leader recently taught everyone the song:

> 'Great, great, brill brill, wicked, wicked, skill, skill
> To have a friend like Jesus'.
> Doug Horley

Many of the adults found it difficult to use the word, 'wicked' in that context, but everyone soon discovered that it meant 'great' and learnt it complete with actions! Over the next couple of weeks, we discovered that the children were singing it in their school playgrounds and teaching it to their friends. I even heard that it was sung in a school assembly.

Children are also very sensitive to the Holy Spirit. One Sunday morning there were about seventy or eighty of them in front of the platform. We were singing an intimate worship song and there was a wonderful stillness over the meeting. As the musicians played, I told the children about Samuel and how God spoke to him. I said that if they had listening ears, God could speak to them too. The worship time could have been considered 'adult' but the children were incredibly sensitive to the Spirit. Many of them were trembling under the power of God, some were on the floor, while others were praying for one another.

I want to include children as much as possible without being childish or gearing our meetings towards them. I'd encourage parents to involve their children in worship. If parents and children worship together at home, the children will slip easily into worship in the context of an 'adult' meeting.

What do you do about people who are hurting?

You'll always have people who are hurting in a congregation. You can be moving powerfully in spiritual gifts — under adrenaline as well as anointing, but it's important to remember that not everyone is where you are. God is a comforting God, so at some point in a worship time it's good to encourage those who are going through difficulties.

The early church worshipped in homes, but where do we see congregational and celebration meetings?

Although congregational meetings aren't specifically mentioned in the New Testament, it seems likely that the early church used the synagogue model of worship and developed it. Celebration meetings are also implied in Scripture. In Acts chapter 5 the Christians worshipped in Solomon's Colonnade, which stretched along the east side of the temple for 480 metres and was over 40 metres wide at its narrowest point. Such a vast area would have held thousands of people.

Does worship leading differ according to the size of group?

Yes. You must know what kind of meeting you're in, because the dynamics are different in the three sorts of meeting. In my experience a congregational style meeting functions best with up to 200 people and a celebration over that number.

Some people think that cell group worship should be quite formal. They assume that they need song books and musical instruments. But some of the best worship times that I can remember were in prayer meetings when there were neither books nor instruments. We just worshipped freely, sang in the Spirit and met with God. Sometimes it helps to sing with instruments, but there can often be a greater degree of spontaneity without them. The worship at this kind of meeting should flow fairly freely. If you come unstuck and it goes off course, it doesn't matter too much. You're not in a public setting so you can stop, talk about it and pull it back together.

What about leading a congregational meeting?

The emphasis in congregational meetings is participation through the spiritual gifts. If you're the worship leader, you're rather like someone standing on a punt. You push the pole against the bank and let the current take the punt. Then you use the pole to steer it round a bend or push away an overhanging branch. You start with two or three songs, but then stand back and let the congregation set the tone of the meeting.

Leading a congregational meeting is difficult because of its unpredictability. The people need to be confident that you'll lead effectively and bring a sense of harmony to what's going on. This requires the kind of sensitivity which knows when to interject and when to remain silent.

And celebrations?

These are really awesome and exciting to lead — especially when people really want to worship. You can feel as though you're at the controls of a powerful racing-car — one touch on the throttle and you're away. Like the car driver, you need to harness and control the power at your fingertips, knowing when to brake, when to accelerate and when to change gear. You have to time things to perfection to gain maximum performance.

There's latent power in a large congregation of worshippers. Your job is to gather the people and harness that power. You don't manipulate them, rather you listen to the Spirit and encourage them to release the worship that's already in their hearts. You really need to give a firm lead both to congregation and musicians alike.

What qualities do you need to lead a celebration meeting?

First, a sensitivity to the Holy Spirit. People naturally get excited when they're worshipping together, but excitement mustn't be confused with God's presence. Don't stir up people's emotions artificially by using things like hand-clapping to liven up the meeting. Rather, focus people's attention on God, then they'll worship with understanding. Emotion will then spring naturally from what they know.

Second, prophetic anointing. You need to know what God is saying to your generation and choose your songs to fit in with this. Of course, all the Scriptures are relevant all the time, but there are seasons when God focuses the church's attention on a particular aspect of the truth — like fellowship, spiritual warfare, building the church, or the reign of Christ and the establishment of his kingdom. You need to be able to lead out in prophetic songs too — which means that you've got to have good clear voice, the confidence to pitch a song and an ability to hold a melody line.

Third, confidence. You set the tone for the meeting so you must give a confident lead from the moment you stand on your feet. Give clear and precise instructions, but make people feel relaxed too. Be aware of practical problems like bad acoustics, and don't let an indiscriminate tambourine player dictate the tempo. Keep the musicians and congregation in time with a simple hand motion if necessary. But don't overdo this or you'll draw attention to yourself.

The main problem with celebration meetings is keeping a sense of flow. You need to know how to move on from one part of the worship to the next as easily as possible. The biggest mistake is talking too much between songs — the people end up listening more to you than worshipping God. If you link songs together, you shouldn't need to bring more than the occasional comment. Plan the worship time and get a sense of what God wants to say and do in it. Then be willing to let him interrupt and introduce something different.

Can individuals use spiritual gifts in celebration meetings?

Participation in celebration meetings will obviously be more corporate than individual — singing, dancing, shouting, clapping, that sort of thing. But I like the idea of getting people to interact with one another in the celebration meeting. I see no reason why you shouldn't divide a very large company of people into groups of about ten each and encourage them to sing psalms, hymns and spiritual songs to one another. They could also pray together, minister healing and prophesy to each other.

You always seem so confident when you lead worship. Is this always the case?

No. Sometimes I go away from worship meetings wondering if I've got it right. I have to battle through these feelings because I know that I've got an enemy who hates worship and will do everything he can to stop people praising God. Tensions often come before a meeting even starts. Maybe I can't find the music for a song, or the P.A. isn't working properly. Then the devil can get in and disturb my peace. That's why I pray with a worship band before we start rehearsing. We don't want to be overwhelmed by niggling problems, but to be conscious of the presence of God. The enemy comes against us after the meetings too. So if you're a worship leader you must recognise that you're in a battle and resist the enemy onslaughts.

CHAPTER 13

CONNECTING

with our CULTURE

S everal years ago Rosie and I took our two sons, Luke and Nathan, on holiday to Menorca. While we were there, we met a couple who were of similar age to Rosie and me, but who had no children. They were fascinated by the dynamics of our family life and we had many meals, social times and interesting discussions together. We thoroughly enjoyed their company and continue to send them postcards when we're on holiday.

What struck me about our friendship was how similar and yet how different we were. The similarities were: background, education, professional status and age. The main difference was this: we were Christians and they weren't. This difference wasn't just a matter of belief in God — which they probably had. It was more to do with the fact that he was our life. Whenever we discussed a topic — whether politics, education, or leisure — we came at it from a supernatural angle rather than from a material world view. Everything we said or did was based on our love for and our knowledge of God.

I don't think Christians realise how wide the gulf is between believers and unbelievers. Our society has little Christian basis to its culture, education system, or philosophy of life, so it's not surprising that people don't easily understand our values. If we're going to fulfil the great commission to preach the good news to every creature, we must find a way of bridging the gulf, of presenting the message of salvation so that people can accept or reject it.

ARE WE DOING THE GROUNDWORK?

In the parable of the sower, the seed is the message of the kingdom and it falls in four different places. Some falls on the path and the birds eat it. Some falls on rocky ground where the plants start growing, but are withered by the sun. Some falls among thorns which choke the plants. And some falls on good soil where it yields a harvest. Good ground needs good preparation.

I often wonder if our evangelistic efforts would be more successful if we gave more attention to preparing the ground to receive the gospel. Many people have no supernatural world view, so maybe we need to do more than preach to them in open airs, knock on doors and give out tracts. Such a confrontational style of evangelism may succeed more in alienating people from us than drawing them to Jesus. Certainly, the gospel is confrontational, but perhaps we confront unbelievers too soon. It's possible that they don't so much spurn the good news as our feeble attempts at communicating it.

Of course, the gospel message does have a power in itself. God is sovereign in salvation and there are seasons when he opens people's eyes to the truth. In times of revival, his Holy Spirit invades our evangelistic methods and brings supernatural revelation. But we mustn't use this as an excuse to neglect an important biblical principle that has clearly been borne out in history: good seed needs good ground in which to grow.

There were 3,000 people saved on the day of Pentecost and another 5,000 soon afterwards. But before this great response to the gospel, Jesus spent three years doing the groundwork — preaching, performing miracles and teaching his disciples. When Paul went to Athens, he had to break into an alien culture, so the ground needed different preparation. The Welsh revival of 1904 saw 100,000 people saved. But the ground was ploughed with prayer and witness long before it began. We live in a pagan society and must ask the question, 'How do we prepare the ground for the seed?'

An important key to this lies in our understanding of the gospel of the kingdom. In the end the salvation message brings about a head-on clash between two kingdoms, but if this clash comes before the ground has been prepared, the seed won't grow. Jesus went everywhere spreading the good news of the kingdom of God. He spent time with people and told them stories. Sadly, we've often narrowed down our evangelism — simply confronting people with the basics of the gospel without recognising the breadth of the kingdom. We've wanted decisions, so we've neglected the ground preparation. An instant society has affected the church.

There's no simple answer to the question, 'Why aren't people being saved faster?' God will respond to our prayers and witnessing. But we must understand his wider purpose for the kingdom. The kingdom is far greater than the church. It's eternal and yet won't be complete until Jesus returns. It's both in heaven and on earth. It's the dynamic rule of God in our lives. It's also the demonstration of that rule in society. The church is the instrument which brings in the kingdom. Jesus told kingdom parables. For example, he said:

'The kingdom of heaven is like yeast that a woman took and mixed into a large amount of flour until it worked all through the dough' (Mt 13:33).

The principle here is that the righteous influence of people can effect change — so maybe we need to focus more on this in our evangelism. We can bring the rule of God into all areas of life — which is why it's important to have Christians in education, politics, trade and commerce, the media and the arts. We're the salt of the earth and one property of salt is that it restrains corruption. So how can we bring the gospel of the kingdom into a culture that understands nothing of godliness? Let's go back to first principles and see.

A CREATIVE GOD

In the beginning, God created everything for his own pleasure and it was all very good. He made the material universe — landscapes, creatures and planets. And he made sound — the wind rustling in the trees, the gentle lapping of the water on the beach and the soft pad of footsteps on the ground. Adam and Eve heard the sound of the Lord as he walked in the garden. God gave man authority to rule over creation — not just the animals, birds and trees, but the sounds too.

God's creativity extended beyond making sound. He also enabled it to have shape, movement and expression. The result is music — a sequence of sounds arranged to form a melody, combined with other sounds to give harmony, moving in a definite time pattern called rhythm. Music is:

'the art of combining sounds of voice(s) or instrument(s) to achieve beauty of form and expression of emotion.'

The Concise Oxford Dictionary of Current English, edited by J. B. Sykes, 1983, by permission of Oxford University Press.

So music was originally God's idea and the first music was probably heard at creation when 'the morning stars sang together and all the angels shouted for joy' (Job 38:7).

Satan isn't a creator; he's a destroyer. He can't create things, but he can pervert what God has made. When man fell, his creativity became perverted and he began using his creative powers to worship man rather than God. He became an idolater. This is true of the visual arts, the written arts, and the aural arts — such as music. A creative God has given man the ability to create music — which is neither good nor bad in itself. But man has used it for evil purposes.

The arts speak of creativity. True art doesn't focus on the artist, but on the Creator and it brings glory to him. '[God] provides us with everything for our enjoyment' (1 Tim 6:17). He gave us the beautiful melodic sound of the flute, the warmth of the strings, the sombre tones of the woodwind and the exciting throbbing sound of the drums, the bass guitar and electric guitar. As his kingdom advances, he recovers music — and the arts — for himself. And music is a powerful force in shaping the way that people think.

MUSIC AND CULTURE

The way in which music affects moral thinking can be illustrated from the 1960s when the Beatles came onto the pop scene. At first, there was a freshness and vitality to their music. It was rooted in rock 'n roll and it captured the imagination of the youth of Britain and America. The Beatles became so famous that John Lennon stated, 'We are now more popular than Jesus Christ.' With this popularity came a spiritual search. The group began to explore things like transcendental meditation and drug taking, and many of their songs started to undermine the moral fabric of the day. Initially people enjoyed their music, but later they were drawn into various philosophical ideas which opened the door from the Swinging '60s into the Promiscuous '70s. Now pop singers can put any ideas across in their music. The devil has certainly perverted music to his own ends.

In the late '60s, songs of protest affected the way that people were thinking. The Vietnam War prompted many Americans to question the rightness of sending thousands of young men to their deaths. Many folk singers made this a theme for their songs, among them Tom Paxton. As students, we used to listen to our Dansette Conquest record players and sing along to his song, 'Lyndon Johnson told the nation.'

The music was popular and the words got into the hearts of the young American intellectuals who formed a pressure group on the American government. They highlighted the evils of the Vietnam War and demanded that something be done. Paul Simon's song, 'A Church is Burning' told the story of the burning down of a negro church by the Klu Klux Klan. It was popular for its musical style, but it also focused people's attention on the evils of the colour bar in the southern states of North America. Bob Dylan's song, 'The times they are a changing' brought a transition from old values into a new way of thinking and behaving.

The arts both reflect and change culture. Aristotle said, 'If you give me a nation's music you have given me the nation.' In the early '60s, Pa Winan of the gospel group, the Winans said to Martin Luther King, 'If you preach it, we'll sing it.' So pop culture began to affect what people thought morally, socially and politically.

CHALLENGE FROM HISTORY

While I was at a John Wimber worship conference, Ron Allen from the Vineyard said that the Beatles gave people a genre of music by which they could worship God. He added that what was going on now was a great recovery process. Certainly, the Beatles did change the whole course of pop music, influencing what would happen through the '70s and '80s and even on into the '90s.

God has given us a cultural mandate — to bring in the kingdom of God by being a righteous presence wherever we are. If we're going to communicate the gospel to people who are culturally alienated from us, we must relate to them through a culture with which they can identify. Music is an important aspect to that.

If music really does affect what people think, maybe it's time that we ploughed the ground of our nation with Christian music. Maybe our church worshipping style should relate to what's going on outside. Of course, everything we do is an act of worship and should give glory to God. But if he created music and if music cuts into the heart of our cultural life, then the way in which we worship will be important in reaching the lost.

Church history tells us that the music of the people communicates the gospel most effectively. So Charles Wesley borrowed Handel's 'See the Conquering Hero Comes' from the Oratorio, *Judas Maccabees* and changed the words to, 'Thine be the Glory, Risen, Conquering Son.' And the song, 'Raise up your Glass for Wine Inspires us' from *The Beggar's Opera* became 'Thou who wast Rich beyond all Splendour.' These songs bridged the culture gap because they related to the people.

Music and the arts can prepare the ground for the seed to be planted, to create an environment where confrontational evangelism can be effective. The troubadours took Martin Luther's songs into the taverns to prepare people's hearts for the preaching of the gospel, and the Salvationists did the same through their brass bands. These bands were of such a high standard that they gained musical credibility and spoke to the society of the time. When George Marshall's band played in the open air, people came out of the pubs to listen.

Today, brass bands have a minor following, but they aren't really part of our culture. The more popular music is generally rock. It fascinates me that when I go into an Indian or Chinese restaurant where I live, I'll hear Indian or Chinese music being played. But if I go into an Indian restaurant in Bombay, I'll hear western contemporary music. When I was in Taiwan, I walked down the main street of Tai Pei and all the boutiques were blasting out western rock music. Yet in a church in Taiwan they were still singing Sankey and Moody which sounded very dated.

I believe that the development of worship music is actually going to help us to relate with our culture. While we mustn't lose people's ethnic identity, there is a music that is broadly accepted around the world. The term, 'rock music' embraces a wide variety of styles and will appeal to different age groups. But there are certain criteria that identify music as rock. The use of a basic rhythm section with bass and drums is the foundation of rock music, whatever the style. So maybe Ron Allen was right and that there is a genre of music that is going to help the world to worship God.

MUSICIANS RESPONSE

God is a creative God who has imparted creativity to his people. I believe that it's time for us to praise him for his creativity by taking our music into the market place. The words of our songs can speak to the heart of our society and show people that there's an alternative way of living. We need to be sensitive to the Holy Spirit in this. We don't necessarily have to present the whole gospel, but we can be a godly influence, witness where we can and prepare the ground for others to preach the gospel. Paul said:

> *'Whatever is true, whatever is noble, whatever is right, whatever is pure, whatever is lovely, whatever is admirable — if anything is excellent or praiseworthy — think about such things' (Phil 4:8).*

Many Christian musicians are doing just this. Instead of writing and singing songs about drugs, sex and the occult, they're writing and singing about the love and power of God — not necessarily in a confrontational way, but in a way that breaks the ground. They aren't producing contemporary songs just to make the church sound more relevant. Rather, they're using their skills to worship God, to communicate with their culture and to proclaim the kingdom.

Worship music is beginning to relate with our secular culture. The musical style of many of the latest worship albums is very similar to that on secular albums. On my album, *Awaken the Nations* the song, 'He has been given' has a reggae arrangement, and the song, 'Eternal Covenant' has a Latin beat. There are strong jazz influences too. Many worship leaders are now using these various influences from the world of pop and rock. Their music is communicating with the unchurched. People hear Christians worshipping to the same kind of music that they hear on their televisions and radios and are attracted by it.

Musicians often have to face the prejudices that people have towards different styles of music. One particular debate revolves around the use of drums, so-called demonic rhythms and certain instrumental sounds. The volume at which the music is played is also thought to be unsuitable either for worship or as a means of communicating the gospel.

We must beware of value judgements based on our cultural background, taste, or religious upbringing. We must also beware of thinking that Satan has creative powers. He doesn't. All he can do is pervert God's creativity. God loves creating music and listening to it. Music is his gift to us. The crucial issue isn't the style, but the spirit in which we're playing it. If we're free from sin, we can enjoy making music whatever the style — because God created it.

When I went to Canada I was overwhelmed by the beauty of the Niagara Falls. But I was most excited when I walked through an underground passage and came out on a platform under the waterfall. The physical sensation was phenomenal — very similar to the physical sensation you get at a heavy rock concert when the vibrations run through your body. Not only did God make the sight of Niagara, he also made the sound of it. The idea that certain worship styles are more appropriate than others really doesn't hold water!

MUSIC AND EVANGELISM

I believe that a kind of worship music is being developed which glorifies God and reaches the lost. Several scriptures link worship with the nations coming to God.

> *Psalm 22:27–28 says, 'All the ends of the earth will remember and turn to the LORD, and all the families of the nations will bow down before him, for dominion belongs to the LORD and he rules over the nations.'*

> *Psalm 68:32 says, 'Sing to God, O kingdoms of the earth, sing praise to the Lord.'*

> *Isaiah 45:22–23 says, 'Turn to me and be saved, all you ends of the earth; for I am God, and there is no other. By myself I have sworn, my mouth has uttered in*

*all integrity a word that will not be revoked: Before me
every knee will bow; by me every tongue will swear.'*

*Isaiah 66:23 says, '"From one New Moon to another
and from one Sabbath to another, all mankind will
come and bow down before me," says the LORD.'*

*Revelation 15:4 says, 'Who will not fear you, O Lord,
and bring glory to your name? For you alone are holy.
All nations will come and worship before you, for your
righteous acts have been revealed.'*

It could be that the worshipping church will create the right
environment for the end time harvest which precedes the
coming of Jesus. Perhaps music and the arts can prepare the
ground to receive the seed. Psalm 40:3 says, 'He put a new
song in my mouth, a hymn of praise to our God'. That's
worship. Then the Psalm goes on, 'Many will see and fear
and put their trust in the LORD.' That's harvest.

Music can open doors to get us into situations where we
wouldn't normally find ourselves. It can also lead to a fairly
direct presentation of the gospel. Kate is a gospel singer and
Mark, a keyboard player. Together they take the gospel into
jazz clubs. One night they were in a jazz club in Brighton
and they performed the old hymn, 'Just as I am, without one
plea' in a style that was very much in keeping with the club
atmosphere. People were there to enjoy themselves, but as
Kate sang, a sudden stillness came over the place and the
words seemed to impress themselves on the audience.

MUSIC AND GODLY INFLUENCE

A direct presentation of the gospel — in clubs and on the
streets — can be very effective, but there's also a way of
sharing the gospel which I'd say was more integrational than

confrontational. It applies to all the arts, but I'll illustrate it from music. It's where musicians develop their skills and write excellent words and music which come from a Christian world view. Their aim is not necessarily to preach, but to be a godly influence wherever they are and to prepare the ground for the seed.

For a long time I wanted to have a band which would fulfil this vision. Then in January 1994 I got some gifted musicians and singers together and started a band called Purple Phat Fish. Each member of the group has a heart for God and a similar musical vision — to be involved in the contemporary music scene, play in clubs and pubs and maybe produce an album which would bring a Christian presence into a secular society. Bands have tried to get record deals in the past, but they've often tried to persuade Christians to buy their records to make them sell. I prefer to see music standing in its own right and people buying it because it's good.

The Phat Fish band write songs that explore subjects like drug taking, premarital sex, abortion, homelessness and social problems. These songs don't all have an overt gospel message, but they do come from a Christian world view. They ask a lot of questions and their goal is to intrigue people. Jesus didn't always go straight for the jugular. Sometimes he just intrigued his hearers — maybe with parables — and left them asking questions.

So the band go into nightclubs and play good music. They don't confront people with the gospel, but they have opportunities to speak about their faith in God. One night while they were playing, someone went up to the sound engineer and said, 'What is it about this band? There's something different about them. It seems like they're all in a kind of family. What is it?' The question opened the door for the engineer to share the gospel.

A well-known local night club owner began to take an interest in the band. He liked their music and soon discovered that they were Christians. The band didn't try to nail him to the floor with the gospel. They just respected him, but their friendship began influencing him. After a while he started justifying his behaviour and saying things like, 'I'm trying to give up swearing.' He's now heard them play in a Christian setting and they've even prayed with him. He still isn't born again, but there's a significant influence on his life.

The band were playing at one nighclub which was packed. Some people arrived and were about to come in when one of them said, 'I'm not going in there, the atmosphere's too good.' When they were questioned about this, it was discovered that they were heavily involved in the occult and had sensed a purity in the nightclub atmosphere. The band weren't going to preach or give testimonies. They were there to entertain, but their presence was having an influence on others.

Of course, the band isn't out to water down the truth. In the end the gospel has got to be confrontational and there's no substitute for gospel preaching. The Phat Fish vision is simply to cross the cultural differences between Christians in the church and those outside it.

When the various expressions of the arts are dedicated to glorifying God, they can communicate with a hostile, non-Christian world. Art exhibitions, dance, theatre and drama — as well as music — can all help in the 'ploughing' process.

WHERE'S IT ALL GOING?

The church needs a broader vision of worship. Worship isn't just limited to Sunday meetings, it's to do with our relationship with God and embraces the whole of life. God originally gave Adam a mandate to rule over the lower order of creation, but

Christians have turned away from that. Instead of infiltrating our culture, we've allowed the devil to rule over it. I believe that through music and the arts, God is helping us to cross the cultural divide and relate with ordinary people — just as Jesus, the friend of tax collectors and sinners, did.

This idea of infiltration need not apply only to contemporary music. There's a breadth of musical appreciation today — illustrated by the fact that the three tenors: Pavarotti, Carreras and Domingo can perform to packed audiences and even top the charts. Children often have opportunities to learn orchestral instruments at school, and the annual *Schools Prom* at the Royal Albert Hall is always a very popular event.

I once had a 'Come and Sing the Messiah' day for people who enjoyed singing. About 150 people — young and old, Christians and non-Christians — came together for a day and worked hard on choruses from *The Messiah*. In the evening we put on an informal concert, complete with orchestra, and performed what we'd rehearsed.

The day didn't just have musical value. The Christians in the choir found that the combination of Handel's great music and the words of Scripture were a great vehicle for worship. And it didn't go unnoticed that they actually believed what they were singing. They had excellent opportunities to relate with others and to share the gospel in a non-threatening way.

I've had the same dentist for many years. I often tried to witness to him — but he was always either cynical or totally disinterested. I knew that he enjoyed good music, so when I put on 'Summer Serenade', a classical concert, I invited him along. He came, and I was delighted to see him in the audience. We included piano music, a violin sonata, a brass group and a chamber choir. The performers were all Christians and the standard was excellent.

At my dental appointment the next day I asked my dentist if he'd enjoyed the concert. He gave a very positive response and then asked why there was such an excellent atmosphere in our church. What was different about the people there? I shared the gospel with him for the next hour.

It's time for God's people to recover the arts for God's glory. I want to see Christian musicians creating good music which declares God's righteousness and performing it well in a non Christian context. Their music can communicate the gospel directly to people's hearts, but it can also speak of God just because it's creative. He gave us beautiful flowers, birds, butterflies, trees, waterfalls, rivers, surf and snow and they all declare his glory. So if his creativity speaks, so can ours. Tozer said:

> *'If the Holy Spirit should come again upon us as in earlier times, visiting church congregations with the sweet but fiery breath of Pentecost, we would be greater Christians and holier souls. Beyond that, we would also be greater poets and greater artists and greater lovers of God and of His universe.'*

Whatever Happened to Worship? by A. W. Tozer, © Christian Publications Inc. 1985, published in the UK by OM Publishing, Carlisle.

I'm looking forward to the day when God's glory fills his temple. I long to see Christians coming together to worship God in a variety of ways which identify with the outside world. Through our music, we can plough the ground for the evangelists to preach the gospel with power, signs, wonders and miracles. We can break down cultural barriers and open the gates for a great harvest to be reaped. We can worship towards revival and prepare the way for the coming of the Lord.

Other titles in the Kingsway Classics Series